Praise for *Your Gui*

"In this book, Amos Clifford offers a delightful introduction to the healing power of forests—and to the natural world that supports wellness in our stress-filled society."

—**Yoshifumi Miyazaki**, PhD, Chiba University, Japan, forest medicine researcher, and author of *Shinrin Yoku: The Japanese Way of Forest Bathing for Health and Relaxation*

"John Muir once said, 'between every two pine trees is a doorway leading to a new way of life.' Now Amos Clifford has given us a beautiful and inspiring guide inviting us to seek out the trees and let the healing happen, both for us and for our beleaguered ecosystems. Grab this book and head outside."

—**Florence Williams**, author of *The Nature Fix: Why Nature Makes Us Happier, Healthier, and More Creative*

"A joyful and insightful invitation to reconnect with forests. Amos Clifford is an outstanding guide to deepening our relationships within the community of life."

—**David George Haskell**, author of *The Songs of Trees* and Pulitzer finalist, *The Forest Unseen*, professor, University of the South

"In this book, Amos weaves a precious tapestry of practical details, poetic imagining, and historical perspective on the practice of forest bathing. It's a delightful read that leaves you yearning for intimacy with nature."

—**Sylvie Rokab**, award-winning filmmaker, "Love Thy Nature"

"If we are to survive and, hopefully, thrive as a species, Amos Clifford's book is a must read. Clear and insightful, his writing is pure poetry. Our relationship to Nature can be renewed and Forest Bathing shows us how."

—**Rosita Arvigo**, author of *Rainforest Home Remedies* and *Sastun: My Apprenticeship with a Maya Healer*

"As an integrative internal medicine physician, it's exciting for me to see the scientific data confirming the mental, emotional, and biophysical benefits of forest bathing. However, what makes this book so excellent is how Amos Clifford describes the experience of forest bathing in a way that is so poetically engaging. His writing unites us with the healing rhythms of nature to bring about a profound peace of mind and heart."

—**Philip Barr**, MD, Duke Integrative Medicine

"In these pages, Amos Clifford asks: 'Remember watching clouds as a child, seeing the shapes of fantastic creatures appear and then morph slowly into something new? I wonder how many adults will do this again, someday, when they are not too busy?' I hope you are not too busy to pick up this poetic and comprehensive book. Take this invitation to revisit a world you may have abandoned as a child."

——**Melanie Choukas-Bradley**, ANFT certified forest therapy guide and author of *The Joy of Forest Bathing, A Year in Rock Creek Park,* and *City of Trees*

your guide to
FOREST
BATHING

your guide to
FOREST
BATHING

Experience the Healing Power of Nature

M. AMOS CLIFFORD

Founder of the Association of Nature and Forest Therapy
Guides and Programs

RED WHEEL

This edition first published in 2021
by Red Wheel Books, an imprint of Red Wheel/Weiser, LLC
With offices at:
65 Parker Street, Suite 7
Newburyport, MA 01950
www.redwheelweiser.com

ISBN: 978-1-59003-513-9
Library of Congress Cataloging-in-Publication Data available upon request.

Cover design by Kasandra Cook
Interior design by Kathryn Sky-Peck
Typeset in Weiss

Printed in the United States of America
IBI
10 9 8 7 6 5 4 3 2 1

Gratitude

To all my teachers, mentors, and guides.
To the many forests, landscapes, and waters that have
held and given life to me, my fellow humans, and
our countless ancestors. To the growing global
community of forest bathing researchers and guides—
may our learning journey long continue.

Dedication

To my children, Erin, Mark, and Jamie.
To all those who are yet to be born.
Tend the forests well.
May their abundance and beauty mirror your own.

Thank you

Pamela for your unflagging encouragement,
Sara for the hard work of tending ANFT while
I've been away for travel and writing, and Michele
for your patience and love. Christine LeBlond, Debra
Woodward, and the other staff at Conari Press for
inviting me to write this and for your support and
guidance along the way.

CONTENTS

INTRODUCTION

You carry a forest inside you. It is a mirror within of the great forests of the world. This book is an invitation to bring those inner and outer forests together.

Forest bathing is a practice that belongs in each person's palette of self-care strategies. It is also a powerful path of activism for those who are called to help heal the broken relationships between people and the more-than-human world. Humans are not separate from nature and have no free pass to escape the effects of the traumas we inflict upon it. Healing of people and forests happens together, or not at all. The medicine that brings healing is in the relationship. Forest bathing is a potent tool in this supremely important work.

Like many practices, it is easy to begin, but also like the most satisfying practices, there are layers of complexity and delight in forest bathing that reward us when we make it a regular part of our lives. This book is a guide to get you started.

I will share some of the core methods of forest bathing. I also touch on some of the philosophy. When we are forest bathing, we work with the forest as our partner. One of the key sayings forest bathers return to as a cornerstone of our philosophy is, "The forest has your back." While we must make an effort, paradoxically it is by relaxing into the forest's embrace that we are most likely to receive its benefits. And these benefits are many. Some are discussed in this book, but others await your discovery.

As your partners in this practice, the trees and forests welcome you. They recognize and call to your inner forest. Take a moment right now to remember a tree that was in some way important to you early in your life. Maybe you walked by a ginkgo on the way to school and for one week each autumn it lit the breeze with golden leaves. Or perhaps there was a huge maple hidden away in the woods near your home—a tree that you felt only you knew about. Maybe you'd go there anytime you really needed to be alone. It doesn't matter if you cannot recall (or never knew) the name of the species. What matters is the *connection* you had with that particular tree—the felt sense that is a part of being in relationship. What was your relationship with that tree?

As your tree emerges from the landscapes of your memory, what details do you recall? How old were you at the time? When did you first see the tree? What were the circumstances? How did you and the tree interact? Did you climb it, shelter under its limbs, build a fort in it, harvest its fruits?

What do you recall of the tree itself? Picture its size; the feel of its bark, leaves or needles; how it changed through the seasons. It could be that only now, as you get in touch with the memory of that tree, are you beginning to see new dimensions of the place it held in your life. Filling in the details of your first encounter with a tree, let the memory take the shape of whatever magic your imagination offers.

My earliest memory is of trees. I am in a crib in my bedroom on the second floor where there is an open window. As the sky slowly lightens with the dawn, I hear the trees greeting the morning with song. In a high quavering voice, the oranges begin their dawn chorus: "Oranges! Oranges! We are Oranges!" It is a song filled with great joy. The lemon trees answer: "Lemons! Lemons! We are Lemons!" and their anthem is equally joyous. Back and forth, on that threshold between the night and the new day, they sing. Those songs are the earliest stream of the soundscape of the forest within me. I don't know how I knew that some trees were called "oranges" and some "lemons." My heart is touched with this mystery and how it hints at layers of relationship between people and trees that are beyond the reaches of our cultural imagination.

My singing trees are an example of how trees touch our lives, often in ways that are so gentle and so much "of the moment" that we may not even notice the connection until, in a moment of later reflection, there comes over us an awareness of the fullness of their offering. It is when we look back that we realize the abundance of their gifts. This is the slow, patient nature of trees. When we spend quiet time in the woods, or in a park, or even our yard, our inner trees—the ones we remember as friends from long ago—are there as well. The stirring in our core, the simple glory of the present moment that is rooted in the ecologies of our memory—this is at the heart of forest bathing.

• • •

Forest bathing can be an occasional event, but it is when we make it a regular practice that we realize its full benefits. While we may not be able to get to a forest every week, most of us can find a way to incorporate at least some of the benefits of forest bathing into our lives, through simple ways of continually renewing and deepening our connections to the more-than-human world of nature.

All over the world people are taking up forest bathing to reconnect to nature and to find relief from the everyday stresses of life. They are receiving many benefits and blessings. My belief is that the desire to be in forests and seek solace and healing among the trees is deeply encoded in the human psyche; it's in our DNA. Our species evolved among the trees and in the savanna environments where forests and grasslands meet. Long ago, our bodies learned to benefit from breathing in the exhalations of the trees, that rich mix of freshly minted oxygen and other aerosols that benefit our moods, our hearts, our mental capacities, our immune systems, and more.

The relationship has always been reciprocal: we exhale the carbon dioxide that the trees breathe in. Our forebears learned to tend the trees, to prune them, to periodically burn away the understory of plants before the fuel load endangered the forest. When societies forget how to tend the trees, they start to remove forests, and inevitably deserts appear, springs run dry, weather patterns change. These are the times we are in. Somehow, as a species, most of us no longer know trees as our relations and view them instead as crops to harvest in service of purely human aims.

This is one of the reasons why forest bathing is important for our times. The trees need us now. They call us back into the groves of their congregation with offerings of healing. And we come to them precisely because we remember in our bones the power and beauty and generosity of the trees. We deeply intuit that it is our birthright to recall their songs.

I've experienced forest bathing in many of the great forests of the world. I've walked among ancient oaks in Serbia that rival the size of some of the coastal red-woods in California. I've conversed with the most ancient of bristlecone pines of the high, cold mountains where Nevada and California meet. I've lain on the friendly soil in the New Zealand forests where the kauri stand in their magnificence. In Japan I was held between the roots of a hinoki cypress named "The Ancient One," who shed raindrops from its branches onto my upturned face. I feel most at home in the oak and bay woodlands of the California coastal ranges, because they are where I spent my childhood and where I live today. Among all of these forests, in the company of their trees, I have come to know a quiet transformation of my heart and mind. At first in whispers, and over time in voices more audible, the forests are teaching me to, once again, hear how the singing of the trees is a chorus woven in harmony with the song of my life.

• • •

This book is an invitation to trust your inner forest to guide you into a delightful practice among the trees. Whether you live in the countryside, suburbs, or the city, this book offers you a framework and specific activities you can use to explore forest bathing on your own. I won't make any promises, but I will say this: the experience can be profound, even transformational.

Nomenclature: What's It Called?

The exploration of forest bathing in this book is based on the practice I and my colleagues at the Association of Nature and Forest Therapy Guides and Programs (ANFT) have developed. We refer to what we are doing as "forest therapy." We are inspired in part by Japanese practices, but we don't attempt to replicate their methods, which have developed in a way that is a great fit for unique aspects of Japanese culture. The Japanese term for this practice, *shinrin-yoku*, translates literally as "forest bathing." That is the origin of the title of this book and the term we use most often throughout it. I view the terms shinrin-yoku, forest bathing, and forest therapy as almost interchangeable. There is only a subtle difference, in that forest therapy implies that the practice is taken up with an intentional goal of some type of healing best done with a trained guide. In Japan, besides shinrin-yoku, guides will sometimes describe what they do as "*shinrin*-therapy." The methods they employ are focused on boosting wellness and preventing disease. "Forest bathing" suggests to me a more casual experience among the trees, unburdened by expectations, oriented to simple pleasure.

1

WHAT IS FOREST BATHING?

The word *bathing*, when used with the word *forest*, conjures images of swimming in rivers or lakes that are surrounded by trees. That's rarely a part of forest bathing, but it's not entirely off the mark. The air through which we walk is in many ways similar to water. It moves in currents, it flows in waves; you can see this in the myriad patterns of clouds floating in the ocean of sky. It is inhabited by living ecosystems, from the glittering strands of breeze-borne silk to insects and birds; it carries pollen and wind-borne seed, along with soil and fungal spores. Sound travels and spreads in layered patterns of information. In these ways and more, the atmosphere is much like the ocean. The air around us is an ocean in which we have always bathed.

In the practice of forest bathing we immerse our senses in the special qualities of the fluid, oceanic ambience of the woodlands. We walk slowly so we can focus our senses on the myriad ways the living forest surrounds and touches us. Feel the breeze on your skin; hear the gurgling voices of the brook and the calls of birds; see the movement of trees in the wind. By giving attention to your senses, you turn down the volume on the cacophony of inner thoughts. Your senses bring you into the present moment, where you can take in all the forest has to offer, welcoming it, letting it settle inside you. When the forest is allowed its place within you, it supports your body's natural capacity for wellness and healing.

Forest bathing is not the same thing as hiking. The destination in forest bathing is "here," not "there." The pace is slow. The focus is on connection and relationship. Sometimes when I tell others about forest bathing, they will say, "I have done that my whole life." Maybe—but probably not. Most of us have never learned the art of stillness in nature. There are exceptions: a fly-fisher, for example, learns over many long seasons of practice how to fully tune in to the sounds of the water, the way the sun glints from its surface, the daily and monthly shifting of insect populations and the fish who feed on them. Standing still in the riffles, gauging the currents of air, feeling into the fish and their ways, and casting the line—that slow, sensory feast, in which fishing itself is sometimes forgotten, is akin to forest bathing.

As a child, I had the good fortune to live in a place where there were many woodlands nearby and long trails into the mountains. It was an era of greater freedom for children. In the long unsupervised hours of summer, my friends and I walked countless miles. We did not think of ourselves as hikers, but sometimes that's what we were. As a young man I became a wilderness guide. I traversed great distances in the woods and deep wilderness, sleeping under the stars for a hundred days or more each year. But except in accidental moments of grace when I let go of any thoughts of my destination, I didn't awaken to the power of the places in which I stood. Most of the time, not having learned yet the art of being silent and still, I was not awake to the generosity of the forest. It was only after decades of meditation practice and of experiencing new ways of being in nature, such as vision questing, that I learned to slow down and to pay attention sufficiently to begin a process that has for me been one of *remembering*. I began to remember that I am not separate from nature; that as a human I belong not just to human society, but equally to the society of the more-than-human world. I don't just view its power and beauty from outside, I am *of it*.

Thus, I began forest bathing. In 2011 I began to study forest therapy specifically, and in 2012 I founded the Association of Nature and Forest Therapy Guides and Programs (ANFT). My aim is to share this practice with many others and to help establish it around the globe. I hope that you will share some of the blessings I have received from forest bathing. To bathe in the forest is to be immersed in a grace that permeates the world, to feel an immanent power and beauty that is everywhere, whispering. It is our human heritage as members of the earth community to not just hear these whispers, but to join our own voices to them. If we learn this, perhaps we can begin to undo some of the damage our species has done and find new ways of tending to the wellness of the vast and wild world.

Shinrin-Yoku:
A New Name for an Ancient Practice

Forest bathing has sometimes been called the "ancient Japanese practice of shinrin-yoku." The truth is more nuanced than that. Firstly, the term is not ancient: it was coined in 1982 by Tomohide Akiyama when he was director of the Japanese Forestry Agency. His idea was to develop a unique brand identity, linking forest visits to health and wellness-oriented ecotourism. But this is not to say that forest bathing does not have ancient roots.

Going to nature for healing has a long tradition in many, if not most, cultures. Indeed, until recent industrial times all medicine came from nature in the form of herbs, roots, ritual, and relationships with other beings. The fifteenth-century physician Paracelsus taught, "The art of healing comes from nature, not from the physician." Ancient cities were sometimes designed to incorporate nature for this reason. More than twenty-five hundred years ago, Cyrus the Great had gardens lush with trees built in the Persian capital. Virtually every preindustrial indigenous people had traditions, ceremonies, and rituals, as well as medical techniques, bound to nature and reliant upon it for healing. Many of these were, and still are, forest-based. Where you find traditional peoples and forests in the same place, there will be forest healing practices.

There is a growing surge of interest in these practices, perhaps in response to some of the problematic failures of industrial medicine. Witness the many people who have found value in Ayahuasca ceremonies, a form of forest medicine from South America that addresses physical well-being but also goes beyond it into psychological and spiritual realms. Think of the forest monks who for millennia have depended upon solitude under the trees as a pillar of their pathways to enlightenment. A contemporary resurgence in natural healing practices is flourishing in many countries, under many different names: from *friluftsliv* (or "fresh-air living") of Norway to techniques practiced in German forest spas to *sanlimyok* in Korea, where entire national parks are dedicated to the healing powers of forests. In North America there is a growing network of trained guides who are certified to lead groups on forest bathing outings offered under a variety of names, such as "Nature Wellness," "Forest Mindfulness," and so on.

In Akazawa Healing Forest, near the town of Age-matsu in Japan, I encountered a way in which the ancient and the new exist together. Our guide was Takashi Miura, one of Japan's most experienced shinrin-yoku experts. After a short train ride to the trailhead, followed by a brief orientation, we walked into a lovely forest featuring hinoki cypress, a tree that has strong symbolic meaning in Japanese culture, as well as proven healing properties. At a crossroads where five trails met, there was a closed gate blocking access to one of them. Takashi explained that it led to the sacred site where the first shinrin-yoku walk was held in 1982. But before that event, the place had been held as sacred for hundreds of years. It, like many groves and trees and woodlands around the world, has long been a place where people have found renewal, solace, and healing.

The belief in the healing powers of forests is deeply rooted in Japan, where it is influenced by the traditional religion of Shinto. In the Shinto worldview, all things have indwelling spirits. Mountains, rivers, and also old trees have *kami*, gods or spirits that live within them. Every tree has its *kodama*, a spirit similar to the dryads of

Greek myth. Unseen but felt within the living networks of the land and waters are also the complex ecosystems of spirit. In popular culture they surface in the anime films by Hayao Miyazaki: *Spirited Away*, *My Neighbor Totoro*, and *Princess Mononoke*. These movies, which I recommend to the inner child in every forest bather, are a window into worlds that have long inhabited the collective unconscious of many peoples. Everywhere you go in Japan, from across the street at Shinjuku Station, Tokyo's main rail hub, to the remotest mountain villages, you encounter shrines where kami are remembered and honored. Very often these shrines are for the kami of individual trees, which are carefully tended and to which offerings of small gifts are made. There is an unspoken assumption that sentience exists not just in humans but throughout the natural world.

The Japanese shinrin-yoku guides I have met didn't talk about this while I was with them, and I suppose most of the visitors they take forest bathing don't either. Instead, the Japanese emphasize the scientific rationale for forest walks. Most of the guided walks I've been on in Japan begin and end with measurements of blood pressure and salivary amylase, which are indicators of stress and relaxation. Each forest bather is given a card to write their pre- and post-walk results on. At the end of a walk you can see how your blood pressure and salivary amylase numbers have changed. While the relevance of such measurements as an assessment tool may be debated, the message behind collecting them is clear: "This practice is backed by science."

The approach to forest bathing described here is similar to shinrin-yoku in Japan, but there are also important differences. The Japanese say that they use "all five senses" for forest bathing; but the approach described in this book includes additional senses such as proprioception, body radar, and imaginal communication, discussed in a later chapter. My practice has allowed me to familiarize myself with at least fourteen senses. In forest bathing, they accelerate my connection to nature, self, and others. These additional senses can be tapped into—or more likely remembered—quite naturally through the invitations forest therapy guides use on our walks.

Forest Bathing in North America

When the first Europeans arrived on the eastern shores of North America, they encountered peoples who had lived in harmony with the forest for thousands of years. It was said that a squirrel could travel through the trees from Maine to Mississippi without ever touching the ground. (Presumably, these squirrels were adept at swimming the many rivers crossed along the way!) What remains of these primal forests is still magnificent and inspiring, although greatly reduced. The forests of North America have provided food, medicine, shelter, and, perhaps most importantly, a stable sense of place to their inhabitants. Writers like Thoreau, who came on the scene much later, expressed what many others felt in his essay "Walking": "I think that I cannot preserve my health and spirits, unless I spend four hours a day at least—and it is commonly more than that—sauntering through the woods and over the hills and fields, absolutely free from all worldly engagements."[1] This is clearly forest bathing long before the term existed.

Thoreau lived in times that were much more agrarian, and therefore more connected to natural cycles and the rhythms of the forest. Much of that association has been lost as our cultural consciousness has been increasingly shaped by technology, industry, and an orientation to productivity. We live in a time that calls for a renewal of our ancient relationships to forests.

• • •

The story of forest bathing in North America is shaped in large part by the organization I founded, the Association of Nature and Forest Therapy Guides and Programs (ANFT). Its mission is to develop and disseminate the practice of forest therapy, leading to its widespread acceptance and integration into health and wellness practices and programs and ecoactivism. The taproot of our approach to forest bathing begins perhaps with childhood memories. That first remembering is a type of personal origin story; it is the seed from which we grow into who we become.

I remember the singing of the trees; thus, I have become a forest therapy guide. To me, to be a "guide" means something very specific. It is the task of a guide to support partnerships between people and the more-than-human world. I started exploring this in the 1970s as a young wilderness guide in programs for at-risk youths.

Guiding is seasonal work, and in the off-seasons I developed a career as counselor and a nonprofit leader, earning degrees in organizational behavior and counseling. Thus, from the root of the singing trees of my childhood grew the trunk. Training as a psychotherapist is one of several large limbs coming from that trunk. For decades I practiced Zen meditation—another limb. Yet another is my studies and practice in the field of restorative justice, a way of helping communities and individuals move toward healing after instances of trauma and criminal victimization. I saw how forest bathing can embody restorative justice in our relationship with the land, helping us to hear the voices of the more-than-human world and to understand from its point of view the impacts of the traumas we have inflicted. It helps us to move into new partnerships and mutual healing.

Each of these limbs has its visible expression and its corresponding set of roots.

The tree grows, finding its place in the forest. Its leaves grow and shed with the seasons. Fires sweep through; it is scorched but survives. I imagine you'll find this imagery familiar, that your life has moved through similar cycles of change and growth. If at times we have felt stunted, it may be that we neglected our roots, that part of our ourselves by which we draw sustenance from the land itself; for it is from the land that our deepest lives are fed. The great disease of our industrial civilization is that most of us are no longer connected to the land. No wonder we see so much uprootedness among peoples everywhere.

If we can envision ourselves as patterned on a similar spiritual template as trees, perhaps we can feel our way more readily into the forest. In later invitations I will sometimes dare to speak for the forests, transmitting what I have learned from them in my decades of guiding. What I offer as the teaching of the trees cannot be called science; instead, their lessons feel like stories, arising from the same dreamscape from which comes myth. I hold these stories loosely, allowing them to guide me when my heart tells me that it serves to do so. I invite you to hold the stories you receive from trees in the same way.

Perhaps your forest bathing experience will give you, as it did me, this story as a point of beginning: Forests do not see humans as separate from them. They seem to long for us to return to our ancestral knowing of them. The trees welcome us, and are glad of our returning.

2

THE HEALING POWER OF FOREST BATHING

I have yet to meet anyone who needs to be convinced that forest bathing is beneficial. For most people, it just makes sense. Still, there is such a wealth of discovery about the benefits that I would be remiss to not touch on it here. What follows is a brief glance at some of the highlights.

Simple Relaxation

For some people, forest bathing is simply an enjoyable and relaxing way to spend a day out in nature. There's really no need to make more of it than this. But it can be surprisingly difficult to relax.

Think of the advertisements for vacation getaways with images suggesting long hours in beachfront hammocks. They may be alluring, but not many of us could stand it for long; the compulsion to get up and do something would soon lift us out of the hammock in a restless search for stimulation. Forest bathing can help us learn to relax. Of course, the paradox is that relaxation implies an absence of goals, so as soon as we set relaxation as a goal we're on tricky ground. We can be trapped by our internalized "adultisms" that value the structuring of our time we have learned as grown-ups over the free play of children. We fear "wasting time."

Forest bathing gives us the opportunity to leave such preconceptions behind. Applying them to neither our children nor ourselves, we can just let the moment be what it is. There is no need to rush. There is no need to "make good use of time." There is nothing to accomplish. Simply let the moment be what it is. And take care not to turn "letting it be" into an accomplishment in itself, just another "something" to chase after.

Physical Health and Well-Being of Humans

In a comprehensive review of the pertinent literature, University of Chicago researcher Ming Kuo writes, "The range of specific health outcomes tied to nature is startling, including depression and anxiety disorder, diabetes mellitus, attention deficit/hyperactivity disorder (ADHD), various infectious diseases, cancer, healing from surgery, obesity, birth outcomes, cardiovascular disease, musculoskeletal complaints, migraines, respiratory disease, and others."[2] Nature is a powerful physician.

Significantly, forest bathing provides a boost to the immune system. Counts of "natural killer" cells that attack cancer and harmful pathogens increase after forest bathing, and the ripples of this single effect are wide reaching throughout our bodies. Kuo proposes enhanced immune function as a central pathway for explaining the myriad health outcomes associated with nature: "Nature stimuli are likely to boost immune function by way of their demonstrated effect on parasympathetic activity, and subsequent effects of parasympathetic activity on immune function." The terms *parasympathetic* and *sympathetic* refer to parts of our nervous systems of central importance in this discussion, and we'll return to them later in this chapter.

Another major benefit of forest bathing is an increased sense of relaxation and greater mental clarity. After a few hours of forest bathing we'll likely feel more relaxed. That may mean we'll just feel better overall. We may have greater mental clarity, be more creative, and be more present with those we love. If we are plagued by anxiety or poor concentration, that will improve.

There are studies that have found that some of these benefits will persist for at least a week after a forest bathing excursion, and in some cases up to a month. A regular weekly practice of forest bathing will maintain them and, over time, boost them toward optimum levels—this with no medical intervention, no prescription medications, no invasive procedures.

Our bodies are remarkable self-healing organisms when in a balanced state. It's worth wondering if the forest should be our primary physician, with our doctors in support roles, to be called upon in the increasingly rare instances they are needed.

In a comprehensive review of shinrin-yoku-related research,[3] Margaret Hansen and her colleagues at the University of San Francisco found that there is a large body of robust evidence honing in on several benefits of forest bathing. They agree that the improvement in the overall functioning of the immune system is very significant. They also find converging data giving evidence that forest bathing decreases cardiovascular illnesses, such as hypertension and coronary artery disease. This is hugely significant, as these illnesses are responsible for many deaths.

In more good news about forest bathing, it helps with respiratory system issues such as allergies. The authors concluded that "research conducted in transcontinental Japan and China points to a plethora of positive health benefits for the human physiological and psychological systems associated with the practice of Shinrin-Yoku, also known as Forest Bathing." And all of this comes about at just the cost of enjoying walks in the woods.

Scientists who specialize in this field are actively refining their research methods, leading to increasingly reliable results. I experienced this myself when I visited Dr. Yoshifumi Miyazaki and his team at Chiba University in Tokyo Prefecture at the Department of Environmental and Human Health Science. Miyazaki is one of the leading researchers on forest bathing and his work is widely published in the peer-reviewed journals. He is one of an elite group of legends in the field.

Chiba University is a one-hour train ride from Shinjuku Station in downtown Tokyo. The Department of Environmental and Human Health Science consists of a cluster of low buildings with a persimmon orchard on one side. I arrived on a cool, cloudy day, along with four other American members of our Forest Therapy delegation, to meet Dr. Miyazaki and his team and learn about their research.

He took us into a small laboratory that reminded me of recording studios, with soundproofing panels on the wall and a rack of computer equipment occupying about half of the space. In the other half was a single chair facing a large, high-resolution video screen.

I sat in the chair and the team put an elastic band with two attachment points on either side around my head. Small infrared transmitters were inserted into each of the attachment points, a pair for each hemisphere of my cerebral cortex. These sensors detect fluctuations in mental engagement and excitement, which are recorded on the computers.

The room lights went dim, and the screen in front of me displayed a solid block of gray. Soon a new image appeared: a photo of city skyscrapers. It stayed up for perhaps two minutes, then there was another minute of the gray screen. Then came a forest scene, just a simple still image, predominantly green. Afterward, we all gathered around the monitors to see the results. My brain did indeed respond differently to each scene. This real-time data collection is an example of how Miyazaki and other researchers are working to refine methods using cutting-edge technologies.

Researchers in many countries have been using many tools to increase our understanding of what happens in the body when we are exposed to natural settings. They've monitored how cortisol and amylase levels, both indicators of stress effects on the endocrine system, change when forest bathing. They've looked at blood pressure. They've had participants fill out questionnaires to track how their moods are affected over the course of a walk. There is a sense of engaging in a meta-experiment to find out which set of experiments gives the most reliable data. It's not just a matter of asking the question; it's also figuring out what question to ask and how to do so.

An emerging gold standard for measuring the effects of forest bathing is heart rate variability (HRV), used as a general indicator of how our nervous system is functioning. Since the nervous system is central to our overall health, when it is impaired, a cascade of deleterious effects ripples through our bodies. To appreciate this fully, consider that the human species has lived in wild areas for 99 percent of our history. One of the ways we have adapted to nature is with the two-part structure of our nervous system: the parasympathetic and the sympathetic.

Think of hanging around in a friendly forest where you feel reasonably safe from predators and other hazards. In these circumstances your body is in the "rest and digest" state dominated by the parasympathetic nervous system, which manages the routine duties of breathing, circulation, and the like. When we are in an optimum state of relaxation, the heart beats not like a metronome, but with exquisite responsiveness to subtle, moment-to-moment changes in the environment. Most importantly, the time between beats varies, and this is called heart rate variability.

In contrast, think of encountering a lion at the edge of the forest. Instantaneously, the sympathetic nervous system takes over, and a host of physiological events take place to optimize our bodies to respond to short-term crisis. This is the state we know as "fight, flight, or freeze." One part of this response is that our heart rate ramps up to provide oxygenated blood to major muscle groups and its beat becomes much more regular. After the threat is gone, we quickly recover and return to baseline functioning. If we were to remain in the accelerated state for extended periods, our health would deteriorate.

By measuring HRV, we can make inferences about the current functioning of our nervous system. A parasympathetic state characterized by greater HRV is when our bodies are in health maintenance mode. A lower HRV indicates a sympathetic-dominant state in which our bodies are fixed in crisis mode.

In eras past, our short bursts of fight or flight tended to have one of two outcomes: they ended quickly, or we did. When we survived, our bodies returned to a state where the parasympathetic system was dominant. It is in this state that our self-healing capacities are fully mobilized. But in our current industrial era, stress is endemic. Every day we swim through a toxic brew of environmental poisons, twenty-four-hour news cycles, and high-pressure school and work deadlines. With our bodies chronically in a low-intensity fight, flight, or freeze status, our health deteriorates, and our mood and mental capacities are affected. It becomes more difficult to maintain the relationships and social networks on which our emotional well-being depends.

The toll on our well-being is immense. A whole catalog of stress-related illnesses is linked to this pressure on our nervous system. Separated from the forests that our DNA recognizes as home, disconnected from the land, our species finds itself in new circumstances for which the slow clock of evolution has not kept pace. We have not had time to adapt to the stressed-out world we have created in the short time span of the last century.

But there is good news: Forest bathing resets our nervous systems. It does so quickly and effectively. It is as if we have come home—*because we have.*

• • •

So far, we've been exploring one br oad research question about the effects of nature on human health. A complementary question is, "How do these effects happen?" What physical mechanisms trigger the beneficial physiological changes produced by forest bathing? In her research survey, Ming Kuo has compiled a list of "active ingredients" in nature, ranging from the enriched oxygen emitted by trees to the pleasant sights and sounds, increased exposure to biodiversity, and reduced exposure to violence. This potent medicinal brew sets us at ease.

One much-studied mechanism is the effects of phytoncides, naturally occurring compounds emitted by trees. The word *phytoncides* means, literally, "plant killers," and when a tree or shrub detects a threat from, for example, a fungus, its immune system ramps up their production to control the growth of the infection. Our bodies respond positively to some of these phytoncides, which seem to work in concert with our own immune systems. This makes sense, given that we evolved among the trees, breathing in these very compounds. Phytoncides introduced into pathogens cultured in a petri dish slow, stop, or in some cases destroy them completely. It's a powerful finding.

While phytoncides and their effects are fascinating, many other influences have also been studied. What combination of colors has the most calming effects? The same as those we find in forests. What sounds are most relaxing? The "big three" of the forest—birdsong, trees moving in the breeze, and water running in natural streams—set us at ease. These findings can be applied in the design of office buildings, where incorporating abundant plant life on the grounds and inside buildings has beneficial effects on worker health and happiness. Hospital patients in rooms that afford a view of trees recover more quickly and are discharged earlier.

And there are many more examples, which are beyond the scope of this book. The curious reader may learn more from the resources listed in the back of this book. An understanding of the mechanisms by which nature affects our well-being is still a relatively new field of study. We can look forward to explosive growth of knowledge in the coming years.

Emotional and Mental Health

Margaret Hansen's survey of the scientific literature mentioned above also highlights the following benefits reported by people who practice forest bathing:

- Reduced incidence or severity of depression, anxiety, and other mood disorders

- A deeper sense of mental relaxation

- Increased feelings of gratitude, selflessness, and wonder

A now famous study at Stanford University provides insight into one of these mental health benefits: a deeper sense of mental relaxation, or a decrease in the tendency to ruminate. Rumination is that state of mind where we get stuck on a hamster wheel of repetitive, often self-recriminating, thoughts. Rumination is one of the criteria that may indicate depression. The Stanford study found that rumination decreased among depressed patients when they walked in the forest.

In my own experience, before I started forest bathing, my moods tended to fluctuate widely. If I had had a "mood-o-meter" gauge, its needle would have frequently swung from the green of mellow and happy feelings to the red of general grumpiness. Nowadays, when I forest bathe once a week or more, the needle on my internal mood-o-meter tends to stabilize in the green zone, and its swings are less dramatic. This has been beneficial in my relationships. If I skip forest bathing for three or more weeks, I can start redlining the mood-o-meter again.

Many healers suffer from various forms of burnout, and that includes environmental activists. I count myself among them. Deeply involved in helping others and saving the world, we too often neglect our own needs. A weekly forest bathing walk is an excellent prescription for activists and healers of all types.

Activism in Action

"People protect what they love," said Jacques-Yves Cousteau. Through forest bathing I have fallen in love with the forest. I want others to feel this way too. We can't engender this emotion by imparting facts only. We need to slow down, listen, and receive the forest's nuanced symphony of sensory offerings. Then our hearts can be touched—we fall in love.

Forest bathing is part of an emerging movement to build a global network of lovers of the land. Forests teach us to think differently about the more-than-human world, so we can relate to our shared earth in a fundamentally different way. The dominant mythology of industrial cultures is that humans—and humans alone—possess sentience, the ability to feel and perceive subjectively. We inherit from this culture an image of the natural world as "less-than-human." We see it as separate from us, as a collection of objects to exploit for solely human ends, as if the land and its many species have no right to existence for their own being.

Oddly, in the long history of our species this view is deviant. Almost all indigenous cultures knew at least some nonhumans as sentient, possessed of awareness and capable of intentional action on their own behalf and to benefit others, and having their own form of individuality and personhood. This view extended beyond animals and plants to include rivers, stones, and mountains. Their forms of sentience are seen as quite different from ours, but nevertheless essential to the fullness of the fabric of life. When our blinders are shed and we, too, become aware of sentience in all living things, our view of the world and our place in it shifts. Our new perspective makes us capable of developing relationships that are deeply meaningful and supportive.

For some forest bathers, the practice becomes an invitation to experience the consciousness of the more-than-human world. It is a powerful, beautiful, and radical form of activism. It is radical because it returns us to our roots through a "re-membering" of who we are. Then our actions become imbued with power and beauty, as our lives are increasingly informed by our growing networks of relatedness.

Healthy Forest Ecosystems

Through forest bathing, we become more attuned to forest ecosystems. When this happens, it becomes more difficult to view them as collections of objects to exploit. Most forestry practices view trees as crops. "Sustainable" forestry generally means replanting logged areas with species that are optimal for later profit. What results is a far cry from a healthy forest ecosystem.

Forest bathing connects us with the loveliness of life as it exists throughout the forest. It reminds us of our fundamental partnership with the lands upon which all species depend. Thus, it can provide a set of visceral experiences that reform our understanding of healthy forests.

In various places around the globe, projects are demonstrating the right relationships between people and forests. Afan Woodland Trust near Nagano, Japan, is one. Founded by C. W. "Nic" Nicol about thirty years ago, it has been a living laboratory for remembering the *satoyama* way of living. Satoyama is a term that signifies the special character of the places where mountains and farmlands meet (*sato* means "cultivated," and *yama* "mountain"). For centuries, it also referred to a traditional form of Japanese permaculture. The people of satoyama villages passed wisdom from generation to generation on how to harvest trees, bamboo, mushrooms, and wild herbs and hunt in ways that preserved and even improved the health of the forest ecosystems.

Nicol began with a large plot of crop-oriented forest-land. Using biodiversity as a measure, he noticed that it was impoverished. There were far fewer insect, bird, and mammal species than would be the case in a healthy forest. His project has restored the forest to health. One of many techniques he uses is to pull the logs of cut trees out of the forest with teams of horses, rather than mechanized equipment, because the horses' hooves churn the soil in a helpful way. He has restored waterways, removed invasive nonnative species, and planted with an eye to creating habitat for critters. As a result, the forest has blossomed. Everywhere there is life—a species-rich explosion of diverse color and activity.

Significantly, throughout this forest one encounters places designed for human gatherings. Seated in a simple shelter among the trees, Nicol served our group soup he made of mushrooms he had gathered nearby. People and woodlands belong together.

I feel that this project is a result of Nicol's own journey of deep nature connection, which has involved long periods in wild places as far afield as the African bush and the Arctic tundra. He is deeply attuned to natural cycles and the pain of wounded lands. A natural-born activist, his work is a powerful example of what can be done to heal forests. Forest bathing develops the same kind of deep connection that calls us to action.

Social Connection

Sharing meaningful experiences with others is one of the main reasons people take to the outdoors. Our time in nature is often a great opportunity for conversation and insights that might not emerge in other settings. A challenge when forest bathing is to include conversation in a way that does not distract from the experience. An engaging conversation can quickly take us out of our senses and back into our heads. We can walk for quite a distance without being aware of what is around us.

Yet social connection is important. We need each other's help to develop our capacity for noticing what is around us. Forest bathing does not aim to eliminate conversation, but it does seek to keep it from overtaking our other senses. From time to time we gather in a circle and take turns sharing what we are noticing. Three things tend to happen as we listen to each other. First, we might think, "I noticed that also." Slightly more nuanced is, "I noticed that also, but didn't notice that I noticed it until you shared." Finally, we might think, "I didn't notice that at all!" and our curiosity might be piqued in a way that heightens our sensory awareness.

This form of sharing helps us train each other to become more skillful forest bathers. Choose silence for the walking or sitting periods between shares to contain the tendency to converse. With friends, agree to have three or four times during the walk when you will gather and take turns sharing what you are noticing, while maintaining supportive silence at all other times.

Spiritual Practice and Mindfulness in Nature

Many forest bathers feel that there is a spiritual dimension to the practice. In the forest, it's not unusual to have a "unity experience": our sense of self dissolves and for a moment we no longer experience ourselves as separate from the natural world. Usually, this type of experience seems more real than ordinary reality. These moments feel transcendent, as if they belong to a different realm. When we are deeply attentive to our sensory experience of the world—when we move slowly enough to be truly here, now, they arise quite spontaneously. We may feel an awe and wonder during our forest bath.

Sometimes when I am in the forest, I move into a form of prayer. Speaking to the plants and creeks, the birds and clouds—all the many beings and places—a feeling of gratitude comes over me. It is like a song the forest calls from within my heart; I am compelled to express it with gesture and words. My voice blends with and becomes a part of the voice of the forest. My movements join the living dance in which the trees enfold me. I know a stillness within the dynamic, ever-changing landscape. This is the best way of prayer I have found.

Many forest bathers feel that their time in the woods is a form of meditation. Some call it mindfulness in nature. And mindfulness practice does share with forest bathing an emphasis on sensory experience. The principle is simple: sensory experience is always immediate, unlike discursive (story-based) thinking, which involves us with the past or future or just anywhere that is not here and now. Thus, anytime our attention is focused on our senses, we are being "mindful," because we are present. Forest bathing distinctly emphasizes sensory noticing and deemphasizes heady preoccupations like the familiar naturalist focus on learning facts. In this fundamental way forest bathing is indeed like meditation.

But I suggest caution about trying to fit forest bathing into traditional teachings about meditation, including modern forms like mindfulness. Mindfulness and other meditation practices calm the mind and deepen our connection to the present moment. So far, so good; we're on the same page. But the difference arises in that meditation emphasizes equanimity, in which no experience is considered inherently better or worse than any other. In contrast, on forest baths we particularly welcome pleasure and delight.

Meditators learn to not become attached to any particular state. It took me a long time to understand this. The first decade of my Zen practice was distorted by an idea I held that effective meditation should reliably produce calm, bliss, and insight. It didn't. In fact, a period of meditation was just as likely to be an immersion in anger, doubt, desire, and the whole host of mental and emotional experiences. After several years of particularly intense meditation, I had a pivotal conversation with my Zen teacher. I asked, "The more I meditate, the more brokenhearted I feel. Am I doing this wrong?" She responded: "Amos! How can you be awake in this world and not be brokenhearted?!" That helped set me free from my misconceptions. Doing it "right" is simply being with what is, as it is, without trying to change it. (I'm not saying here that you should be brokenhearted: what was true for me at that time—and often is still—may not be your experience at all.)

As you become more intimate with nature, do not be surprised if you too feel brokenhearted about the harms we humans are inflicting. To cover that sorrow with a forced veneer of bliss would be profoundly dishonest.

You may also feel the sorrow I am speaking of, and perhaps it has been a steady companion for you. Among nature-connection mentors and teachers this is known as the "river of grief," and it seems to be an intrinsic part of the nature-connection journey. At some point in your forest bathing practice you may encounter it. Let the trees help you cross the river of grief. Don't try to take a shortcut. Not always feeling bliss and peace is a part of "doing it right."

We can follow the thread of sensory contact, noticing when it leads us to simple pleasures. When we meet pleasure, we "invite it in." So, for example, when we notice the touch of the breeze on our skin, we might also notice if there is any pleasure in how we feel it. If so, we can give that sensation of pleasure an extra bit of hospitality. Pleasure acts as a gateway to sensual enjoyment. This is not to say that unpleasant sensory experiences are wrong and we should avoid or ignore them. It's a nuanced matter of slightly privileging pleasure when it arises.

One of the mottoes I suggest for forest bathers is, "It's Zen until you say so." Just let the practice be what it is, without extraneous concepts. The moment you say, "This is meditation!" you lose the thread. Trust your senses and the forest to guide you into what is real.

Authentic Relationship with Nature

As a species we have grown increasingly disconnected from the world that sustains us. Many of us never feel the joy of holding a handful of fresh dirt and reveling in its texture and smell. Our disconnect may be so established that we are averse to the idea of coming into contact with "filthy dirt." It's a bit tragic, really. The world would be a barren place without dirt and rain and bacteria and insects. These relatives of ours have made our lives possible.

This disconnection from nature also alienates us from ourselves. When our lives are insulated from the elements and from natural cycles, we become anesthetized, deadened to our senses and finding it increasingly difficult to connect to the sensual processes that allow us to feel joy, delight, and surprise. Our life force is diminished.

Yet an antidote is as near as the closest natural place. Forest bathing is a reliable way to reawaken our senses.

The forest is itself the therapist, restoring our innate capacities when we slow down and give it our attention. It knows what healing we need and how to deliver just the right intervention. The necessary image, the fitting experience, the piercing insight, in the right dose that matches what we are ready to receive: this is what the forest delivers. The methods of forest bathing open the doors of connection so that we can fully receive the healing the forest offers.

This quality of authentic relationship with nature is often missing in the lives of environmental activists and those who work on sustainability projects. Lacking the foundation of a strong relationship, they work as if nature does not require partnership, as if humans can engineer our own way out of the messes we've made. Personally, I doubt it. I think that all of our clever efforts, if conceived and implemented outside of a partnership in which nature informs us, will have subtle flaws that will become their undoing. The deeper layers of forest bathing can teach environmental activists and engineers what it means to partner with the more-than-human world.

3

ELEMENTS OF PRACTICE

Forest bathing opens the doors of our senses and fully engages us with the healing powers of nature. The methods of forest bathing bring our bodies and minds into a relaxed and quiet state, where we are fully aware of where we are and what we are experiencing in the present moment. A simple motto—"The forest is the healer; the practice opens the doors"—is a reliable guide.

Several elements characterize forest bathing and set it apart from hiking and other outdoor activities. One is the *pace*. Forest bathing walks are very slow and relaxed. Another is *distance*. There is no need to go far; often less than a quarter mile will do. (Once a group I was with did our entire three-hour forest bath under and in the branches of a single oak.) Also, we focus on our *senses*. This is a departure from expectations that structured time in the forest should have something to do with learning scientific facts about nature. Forest bathing also invites us to *receive*. We use our senses to welcome the gifts the forest offers us, such as the sounds and sights and unique energies we feel from place to place along the trail. Receiving is a part of *communication* with the more-than-human world. Another aspect of communication, fundamental to a sound forest bathing practice, is *reciprocity*. The reciprocity principle is that we don't just take from the forest; forest bathing is not about humans exploiting nature by extracting wellness and pleasure from it. It is about a *partner relationship*, characterized by communication and give-and-take. *Of these elements, relationship is the most fundamental.* Let your forest bathing practice be a continual inquiry about what it means to be a part of the web of relatedness connecting all living beings. This inquiry is a core *intention* of forest bathing.

The relationships that develop through forest bathing are not something that can be rushed or manufactured. Instead, it is more like a courtship. There is an *optimal flow* of activities that help with this, and we will explore some of these elements in greater detail in this chapter. But first, let's look at important guidelines.

General Guidelines

- Let yourself be guided by invitations, rather than by accomplishing exercises.

- Work with the forest as a partner, rather than as a setting for an activity.

- Your focus should be on a sense of embodiment and vivid sensory experience.

- Minimize efforts to achieve anything.

- Ideally, your walks will last between two and four hours. This allows enough time for the mind and body to slow down and become relaxed.

- You won't go very far, often only a half mile or less.

- With the methods described in this book, use conversation in a minimal but positive and supportive way.

- Your primary goal is not to get a workout. It's more like playtime with a meditative feeling. If you find yourself working out, just pause for a moment of stillness, then proceed again slowly.

- While you can forest bathe in any natural environment, ideally your walks should take place in a wooded environment, with streams and meadows and minimal intrusion from human-made sounds such as traffic or construction.

- The trail should be accessible and easy to walk on.

- Go unplugged, without technological barriers between your senses and the forest. For example, consider leaving your cell phone behind, or only use it in ways that help, rather than hinder, your connection (see the section on "Freedom from the Phone," in chapter 6).

- Don't let concepts such as "mindfulness" or "walking meditation" trick you into making efforts to experience anything other than what the forest offers.

- Don't let the experiences of others or outcomes such as the feelings of awe described in research studies trick you into trying to have those same experiences.

- Let each walk be its own experience; avoid trying to re-create prior positive experiences.

- Trust that when you skillfully open yourself to the forest, it will work with you in a positive way.

- Consider ending each walk with a snack and tea.

Guided by Invitations

Forest bathing follows a series of invitations from the forest. Part of developing your practice of forest bathing is honing your ability to recognize and choose from a constantly shifting kaleidoscope of invitations. Invitations are not exercises or assignments to accomplish. They are not performance oriented. They are more like a flow of improvisational dance, with the forest as your partner.

If you find you are making a big effort to do an invitation "correctly," it's better to just let it go and simply be in the forest. Likewise, if an invitation is intriguing, but the way it has been offered—either in this book or by a guide—is not quite working out, relax and let the forest help you find your way.

Here's where having a "child's mind" is important: playfulness, curiosity, and the willingness to experiment lead us into undiscovered territory, often revealing delightful secret passageways. This book describes many invitations you might try. Exploring these will help you learn how to discover others on your own. Any child can do it—including the child that is alive in you! At the heart of every invitation is a simple encouragement to play.

Sharing Circles: Notice What You Are Noticing

From time to time during your forest bathing experience, take a moment to notice what you are noticing. If you are with others, you can take turns sharing.

Gather in a standing circle and pass a stick or stone around. The rules are simple: The person holding the stick speaks, and the others listen without interrupting. Each person begins with the prompt, "I am noticing . . ." The wording is important. "I am noticing . . ." is more open-ended than, for example, asking, "What did you notice?" It can be approached in many ways. Stick with those exact words as your main sentence starter in most of your forest bathing sharing circles. When finished, the speaker passes the stick to the next person. Take one loop around the circle, and then move on to the next invitation! There's no need to comment on what you or others share; in fact, it's best not to. Just share and move on. Don't give in to the urge to analyze; with an open heart just share what you are noticing. Receive the sharing of others without judgment or analysis, letting their experience be witnessed in just the way they describe it.

If you are on a solo walk with no other people to hear your story, you can share with the forest. Just tell it out loud: "I am noticing . . ." To make it more personal, you can share with an individual tree. Really, almost anything in the forest will listen; just have a playful but sincere attitude. Stones are very patient listeners. Flowers can be light-hearted. Birds may take what you say and spread it as gossip throughout the forest. The important thing is that you feel you have been heard and witnessed in your journey.

More Than Five: Forest Bathing and the Senses

Everyone is aware of five senses: touch, taste, smell, hearing, and seeing. The phrase "all five senses" is so routinely used that we assume that's the full count, but there are many more. Honing our familiarity with the five senses is very important; they are reliable pathways of connection with the world and the present moment. In forest bathing we rely mostly on them, while supplementing them with others that are less familiar.

Additional senses you know already are proprioception and enteroception. When you close your eyes and move your arm, you can sense where it is. You feel your body's location in space. That's proprioception, or the felt sense of embodiment. You also know when you are hungry, when a sickness is emerging, when you need to eliminate, and so on. These sensations are enteroception, having to do with awareness of internal functions. (In contrast, the "five senses" are all categorized as "exteroception," having to do with receiving external information.)

Proprioception is important in forest bathing for encouraging awareness of our body. As with the exteroceptive senses, body awareness is always located in the immediate present. Thus, so long as we are attentive to the movement of our body and the attendant sensations, we cannot mentally be elsewhere.

Beyond these we can also consider four additional senses, some a bit outside the scope of recognition by scientists: mirror sensing, body radar, imaginal sensing, and heart sense, sometimes called "the felt sense of the present moment." These last three are subtle, meaning they are more about an awareness of emotional states or invisible energies than visible or palpable stimuli. They function on the edge where it's hard to know what we are sensing and what we are inventing. Explore them more from a perspective of "interesting stories to play with" than thinking of them as scientifically reliable data sources, although this is not to say they are unimportant. Forest bathers who use them often find that experiences they value most come through these senses.

First, let's look at *mirror sensing*. The presence of "mirror neurons" in humans and other animals has been well established. Their function is not so well understood. One of the leading theories is that the network of mirror neurons within each of us enables us to feel what others are feeling. They may be responsible for empathy and for at least some social learning. In the context of forest bathing, I suggest the possibility that mirror neurons also respond to motion in the environment. Try, for example, watching a soaring bird such as a hawk, eagle, or vulture. When it dips a wing, do you feel that anywhere in your body? How about when a hawk makes a swooping dive while hunting prey?

In the invitation "Walking in Forest Time," we give our focus to what is moving in the environment. Perhaps our mirror neurons are a way of sensing the ambient energy of the forest, as expressed by the velocity and range of branches moving on trees, for example. Does this "mirror sense" then affect us at deeper levels, perhaps shifting our brain activity to calibrate with the energetic "mood" of the forest? If so, it stands to reason that this process will help us more readily connect through our other senses.

This is pure speculation. It's what I call "a good story." It's good, because I like it. It's a story, because it's not quite science.

Body radar is a "knowing" related to something in the immediate environment. It can help us to choose among options. With body radar we detect a source of beckoning, something unseen that is calling. It is perhaps related to the Japanese idea of *chi-sei*, a form of intelligence that is constantly making choices based on environmental cues that are not processed in ways that we normally consider conscious. An example body radar invitation is "Threads of Connection."

We can use the example of listening to trees to help us understand *imaginal sensing*. To listen skillfully to trees, we cultivate the capacity to listen with the whole of our imaginations. We let the presence of the tree and of everything that is happening around and inside of us make impressions on the canvas of our thoughts, emotions, and sensations. We listen with a loose attentiveness, avoiding being carried away by our own skepticism or hopeful projections. In this way of listening, we consider that it is possible that some of what arises in the stream of our minds was generated not from within, but from without. A memory, a daydream, a flash of insight, a sudden urge to move, a wave of emotion—these are a few of the many forms the voice of the trees can take. The movements of the trees, their shapes, and the events that occur in, near, and around them while we are in dialogue may be considered as synchronistic expressions of their voices, which are not separate from the voices of the land. They are responsive and purposeful. And yes, sometimes people claim they hear trees say words, usually with the inner ear but sometimes audibly.

Great artists have honed their capacity to receive impressions upon their imaginations. Van Gogh's painting *Starry Night* is an external representation of the internal impression made by the night sky. His work is a form of communication from the more-than-human world. It becomes personal for each of us when, in our own viewing of the painting, we are aware of the sensory and emotional ripples that course through us. That is one aspect of imaginal sensing.

In forest bathing, anytime we are befriending a tree or in conversation with one or with another nonhuman forest being, we are using our imaginations to receive its message. There are very few people who return from the invitation "Conversation with a Tree" saying they received nothing. I think that for these few, it's a matter of practice and, even more than practice, of simply getting used to the idea that others who receive messages are quite ordinary people. It's a process of normalizing three ideas: that we can be in actual relationship with trees, that trees (and other beings) are imbued with their own forms of sentience, and that through our imaginations we can contact that sentience.

The *heart sense*, also called the *felt sense of the present moment*, is the unique, ephemeral quality of the here and now. No two moments are the same. No two places are the same. A place revisited is not the same place it was on a prior visit. Each time we come to a new turn in the trail, we feel a difference. The location of this sense is in and around the heart. Our hearts are incredibly sensitive and intelligent. We each emit a measurable energy field that extends from our hearts well beyond the boundaries of our skins. This field is constantly interacting with what is around us. The heart field combines with what we are feeling, seeing, hearing, and so on, into a sublime form of knowing.

Explore this sense by pausing from time to time to feel into the question, "What is it like?" For example, "What is it like to be approaching this stream, knowing that I will soon cross it?" "What is it like to be standing where two trails meet?" "What is it like to step from the sunlight into the shade?" Each moment offers its own experience, known by your heart.

It's of great importance that you not answer the question, "What is it like?" When you simply feel the question in your heart, you learn to contact an intelligence beyond words.

Over time I've developed a tendency to naturally and effortlessly feel into the heart field. The ability to dwell without analysis in the felt sense of the present moment now strikes me as a large part of what I have long sought through spiritual practice. I suspect the resulting "softening" of the heart also has physical health benefits.

Sensory Becomes Sensual; Sensual Becomes Intimate

A sensory experience can become sensual we when notice how it affects us: how we *feel*. For example, when we place our hand in a shallow stream, the sensory experience includes temperature, motion, texture, and so on. The sensual experience may be joy, delight, playfulness, or some other "turning on" of inner experience.

Here's an invitation to explore this: Find a tree and engage your senses. First, while looking at it, say: "Outside I see . . .; inside I feel . . ." "Outside I see the tree moving in the breeze; inside I feel pleasure in my belly." Next, touch it: "Outside I feel the rough texture of the bark; inside I feel slightly nervous." Repeat this with smell, sound, and, if the tree offers fruit, taste. The first part is sensory; the second is sensual.

Sensual experience is an essential part of moving into authentic relationship with the more-than-human world. It is a type of communication. Think of sensory input as communication from the world around us. Sensuality is our felt response to the communications received by the senses. A strong floral scent reaches out to us; we are drawn to explore it, feeling sensual pleasure as we bathe in its fragrance. Experiences of this kind are always there around us when we learn to pay attention.

An Ethic of Tenderness

Many people have learned that "leave no trace" is a general ethical principle to follow in nature. I agree that it is a good principle in protected and fragile environments, such as alpine meadows that have very brief growing seasons. However, it is not the ethic I recommend for forest bathing. An alternative is "wild tending." This approach is congruent with the ways of many indigenous peoples, who view the land not as a resource to protect but as a complex web of many relationships, with each being, ourselves included, holding a place of importance and membership. M. Kat Anderson describes this in her book *Tending the Wild*:

> This view of life as related, equal, and highly intelligent is what Enrique Salmon (Raramuri) calls a kincentric view of the world. In this view, nature is not to be treated as a separate entity "out there...." Homo sapiens are full participants in nature, and they share mutual obligations and intricate interactions with many other forms of life.[4]

The heart of this kincentric ethic is the notion of tenderness. Just as we are tender toward the people we love who are under our care, we can be tender toward the forest and its many beings, each of whom are our kin. Our hearts respond to what is happening in the forest, especially as events relate to our own actions. When I am guiding, there is a place where I frequently gather the group to stand in a circle for the invitation "Embodied Awareness." Sometimes we come to that place and it looks a bit trampled. My heart tells me it needs a break, so I take my group to another location. That is tenderness. The forest returns the tenderness it is given. When I return later after giving a location a break, I may be rewarded with a welcoming display of wildflowers.

Forest ecosystems tend to be very resilient in general, but they can also be threatened by thoughtless overuse or by organisms that are either not native or opportunistically take advantage when trees are compromised by drought or other unfavorable conditions. The great kauri of New Zealand are threatened by a soilborne disease; in a very tender response to this, human caretakers have put out water troughs with antiseptics in them, and hikers use these to carefully clean dirt from their shoes before entering the forests where the kauri grow.

Reciprocity

It is a strongly ingrained cultural habit to think of nature as a collection of resources. Forest bathing opposes this assumption. One of the beautiful areas of inquiry in forest bathing has to do with how we can give as much as we receive. We call this "reciprocity practice." If we are not attentive to reciprocity, forest bathing could become just another way to exploit the forests, treating them as resources in service of human health. That is not congruent with the relational aims of forest therapy, in which we respect the gifts offered by all things and expect of ourselves that we will likewise be givers, not merely takers.

Reciprocity increases awareness of the many ways in which we are connected with the more-than-human world. It supports the development of relationships. Aim to creatively practice the reciprocity of both giving and receiving in all your forest bathing outings. You can do this anywhere, at any time, following this simple method:

1. Notice what things exist around you. Either silently or quietly speaking (preferred), acknowledge the thing and describe what you have received from it (and its type): for example, "Here is a tree, which has shared shade and places to rest."

2. Find something to offer it. This could be a gesture or a song; perhaps you would like to write a note and conceal it where only the earth can read it. Allow time for an inspiration to appear.

Learn to incorporate this idea into all your forest bathing activities. It will help to hone your understanding of your relationship to all things.

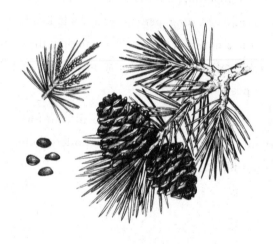

4

FOREST BATHING STEP-BY-STEP: AN OPTIMAL FLOW

The sequence described here has proven over hundreds of walks to reliably create a strong sensory connection with the forest. It brings us home, opening our internal gates and inviting the forest to come meet our minds and hearts and spirits.

It is a framework that provides a predictable pattern with room for flexibility, creativity, and adaptation to circumstances. *Structure* is part of what makes forest bathing a "practice." Its built-in *flexibility* supports our creative capacity to relax into playfully engaging in a nondirected flow of emerging events.

As with any other practice, repetition helps. The repeated use of these invitations will, over time, deepen your understanding and your capacity to fully "drop in." *Dropping in* is a term I've often heard forest bathers use. Its origin is in surfing, a practice that's related in many ways to forest bathing. Surfers wait watchfully for a wave; when one comes, they must paddle to catch it. At a certain point, the paddling gives way to the wave's own energy carrying the board forward. The surfer stands and "drops in" to the wave and the flow of the moment. When your forest bathing practice begins to ripen, like a skillful surfer you will learn how to drop in, allowing the forest and your own embodied awareness to flow together. The optimal flow described in this book will help you understand how to do this.

Overview: Steps in the Optimal Flow

1. Have a firm intention to forest bathe.

2. Begin with a threshold to ceremonially mark the start of the forest bathing walk and set it apart from other experiences. This is called the Threshold of Connection.

3. Stay in one place for at least fifteen minutes, using your senses to explore here, now. The standard invitation for this is "Embodied Awareness."

4. Walk slowly for twenty minutes, noticing what is in motion around you.

5. Choose one to three invitations that are a good fit for the place, the weather, the people, the mood. This part of the optimal flow is called "Infinite Possibilities," because the forest offers many choices. This part can last up to two hours.

6. Sit spot for twenty minutes.

7. Hold a tea ceremony, with snacks and conversation.

8. End with the Threshold of Incorporation, marking the end of the forest bath and your return to ordinary experiences.

1. Intention

Beginning with a clear intention helps prevent the walk from morphing into a hike or a time for conversation. The basic intention can be something like, "For the next two hours I will simply be forest bathing. I will not hike, and I will be silent and attentive to my senses and the forest."

The healing properties of the forest invite us to come with additional intentions. You may have a health care concern; perhaps you wish to boost your immune system because you know that flu season is coming. You may want to realign and balance your nervous system so you can think more clearly and creatively. If you have cardiac disease, you may simply want to relax in a way that supports the wellness of your heart.

You may have a question or relationship quandary for which an answer has proven elusive. Perhaps you have a decision to make, and the options are a perplexing. What if you ask the forest for help? Many times, I've shared a question with a tree at the beginning of my forest bathing walk. Then I just let it go, and stop thinking about it.

Often, at some point on my walk, an answer just pops into my head. I can then pause and give extra attention to my surroundings, offering a moment of gratitude.

Even if you are clear about your purpose at the beginning, it's often still easy to lose the thread. For me, the way this sometimes happens is like this: At first, I move along slowly and attentively, but before long—after say twenty or thirty minutes—I notice that I am simply hiking along thinking about other things. I'm no longer here, now; my thoughts have transported me to the past or future, to some memory or anticipated event. It's important to create a container that will help to maintain present-moment awareness throughout the walk. I've found "thresholds" to formally mark the beginning and end of a walk very useful.

2. *The Threshold of Connection*

A threshold is a place that marks a transition from one place to another. We encounter them every time we pass through a doorway into a room or place that is clearly different from the other side. Often entryways into houses or gardens are given considerable attention to emphasize the transition: the design, the materials, the colors, and the framing may all be chosen with extra care to help define the psychological experience of *entering*.

Using thresholds on forest bathing walks invites the more-than-human world into a partnership that supports the journey. It often seems that using thresholds also stirs the awareness of the forest, alerting it that we are entering with a particular intention. The felt connection with the forest created with a threshold ceremony segues easily into sensing the sentience of the forest.

In the forest there are many natural thresholds. The trail sign at the beginning is itself a threshold; a bridge over a stream marks the transition from "here" to "there." A branch that arches over the trail or even a bend in the path where there is a felt sense of entering the forest would be another example.

Creating your own threshold can be powerful as well. A very simple way to do this is to find a stick long enough to put across the trail. Facing into the forest, put the stick on the ground in front you. Sink into awareness of your body, the place where you are standing, and the special quality of the moment. Bring your intention firmly

Your Guide to Forest Bathing

to mind. Speak it out loud, so the forest can hear. Ask the forest for support. Tell the forest how much time you are committing to your forest bath. Ask it to help you stay safe and present. Humbly offer it your open and soft heart. Express your appreciation and love of the forest, and promise that you will act tenderly toward it.

Pause to listen for the forest's answer. The wind soughs through the branches, a bird calls, a fox shows its face and then disappears into the brush—the forest has many ways of saying: "I hear you. You are welcome here." Finally, step over the stick. Now you have begun your forest bath.

This threshold where you begin your forest bath is called the "Threshold of Connection." Crossing it is a ceremony that supports us as we enter a special *liminal state*, a time "in between" two periods of ordinary life. In Jungian psychology, the liminal state is when our active imaginations are particularly alive. We become receptive to perceptions and experiences that are outside of our normal daily life. These experiences play a significant and necessary role in our personal growth. In liminality, we may escape the rote existence of our "received lives" and begin to contact our unique individual selves.

The conscious use of thresholds amplifies liminality. You don't have to make efforts to produce liminality during your walk. It is automatic, and if you to try to make it happen, you'll only interfere. Relax, don't try to do it right, just bathe in the forest and trust that it will support you.

After crossing your threshold, if you've used a stick move it off the trail where it won't be an obstacle to others. Keep it nearby so you can use it again at the end of your walk for the Threshold of Incorporation. This creates the opportunity for you to feel the special sense of completion when you return at the end, to make your walk a threshold-to-threshold experience.

3. Embodied Awareness

Once we've crossed the threshold of connection and started our forest bathing walk, we give our attention to three things: noticing our surroundings, noticing our body sensations, and noticing how our senses bring us into contact with the forest. The first fifteen or twenty minutes of a forest bathing experience don't involve walking anywhere; we stand or sit in one place. Staying in one place like this establishes a mental framework for the pace of the entire walk. Sometimes so much rich variety is discovered that forest baths never move beyond this starting point.

During "Embodied Awareness" we will scan our bodies and senses, which will prepare us for a fully immersive walk.

Familiarize yourself with these instructions in advance, and don't rush through them. If you are in a group, it may help to have someone read them aloud at a slow pace. You may find that the first fifteen minutes of the walk are indeed a great pleasure.

THE INVITATION GOES LIKE THIS:

Take a few long, slow deep breaths. Notice your body, how it feels to be supported by the earth below your feet. Notice the sky and the other living things nearby.

For the next part, it helps to work with a stone, although you can also do it empty-handed. A well-suited stone is about the size of an apple and has enough mass that some effort is required to hold its weight when you extend your arm. It shouldn't be so heavy that it causes you to strain while holding it in one hand and moving your arms. Its weight will help you to notice the sensations of your bones, tendons, and muscles more clearly.

With a stone in your hand and your feet about shoulder-width apart, slowly move your arms. It can be helpful to reduce visual distractions by doing this with your eyes closed. Reach out to your sides and then in front of you. Take your time and move slowly, always keeping your focus on body sensations. When you hold the stone in front of you, can you trace the ripples of its presence through your muscles all the way to your toes? What happens if you curl your toes; does it send a ripple back? Improvise, playfully trying new ways of moving that help you explore your muscles and bones. This will help you begin your walk with an awareness of embodiment. Do this for two to five minutes, then set the stone down.

Sense of Touch: Eyes still closed, turn your attention to your skin. Notice the ways that the forest touches you. Hold your hands with your palms turned forward, letting them be sensors. Notice the sensations on your skin. Can you feel a breeze? How about temperatures? What does your face feel? Your neck? Are there different sensations in different places? Do the sensations change? Perhaps you notice some way the forest is touching you that feels good, a gift of simple pleasure. Linger with that pleasure; give it your hospitality. Explore the sense of touch for two to five minutes.

Sense of Hearing: What sounds are around you? Notice the variety of sounds. What sounds are nearby, and which ones are farther away? What is the farthest away sound you can hear? What is the quietest sound? Can you detect any patterns or rhythms in what you are hearing? Do the sounds interact with each other? Do they combine, like chords or a symphony? You can exaggerate the sound of your own breathing, just enough so you can hear it blend in with the sounds around you; what is it like to be a part of the symphony of this place? Notice within the experience of sound any pleasure you find. Let that pleasure find a home within you. Listen in this way for at least three minutes before moving on.

Sense of Taste: What tastes is the forest offering in the air that you are breathing? Breathe in deeply through your open mouth, exploring the air as it passes over your tongue. How does the air taste? What is its texture? What does the forest offer you in this moment, in this place, on this day, as you inhale its complex offerings? Perhaps you notice something pleasurable in how the air enters your body. Breathing out, you might wonder how the forest receives your exhalations. Is there something you would like to offer to the forest, carried to it on your out-breath? Can you give pleasure back to the forest? Breathe in this way for at least three minutes before moving on.

Sense of Smell: Breathing through your nose, notice what scents are being offered by the forest. Over the next minute or so, do the scents of the forest change as you explore them? Perhaps move your head from side to side, the way a hound would sniff to track a scent, and up and down, just inviting and noticing. If you crouch down so your nose is nearer the ground, do the scents change? Does what you smell stir up any feelings? Explore scent in this way for at least two minutes before moving on.

Body Radar and Sense of Sight: Eyes closed, hold your hands out to your sides, near your hips, and turn your palms forward. Feel into the direction you are facing with your entire body. As you turn, notice how you feel inside.

Think of your body as having a kind of radar as your feelings register unseen contact in the forest around you. Slowly turn in a circle until you are facing in a direction that somehow feels right to you—the direction your body radar recognizes as a good way to face.

When you are sure about the direction you are facing, slowly open your eyes. Let the forest reveal itself to you as if you have never seen it before. There's no hurry; you can simply gaze for about the time an image taken with a Polaroid camera might take to develop. Imagine that the film is within you, and what is developing is an impression on the film of your imagination. To help develop and embody this internal image, make a physical gesture or movement. Allow this gesture to come as a spontaneous expression from your body, without overthinking it, just moving your body guided by what you feel.

Notice what you are Noticing

After the invitation "Embodied Awareness," take a few moments to notice what you are noticing, as described earlier in chapter 3 using the phrase "I am noticing . . .".

4. Walking in Forest Time

The invitation is simple: Walk slowly, while silently noticing what is in motion in the forest. There is always movement, even when things seem perfectly still. Strands of a web drift in the air, trees move in the breezes, birds fly by, and squirrels scramble in the branches, grasses bend, insects crawl. Creeks are perpetually changing their shape and tune. Inside you there is also motion. Your inner motion cannot avoid mirroring the motion of the world around you, and vice versa. The soothing sound of a breeze will be mirrored within you as calm; in turn, your calm will encourage the squirrels and birds not to flee at your approach.

Until you become accustomed to it, walking slowly for more than a few minutes is, paradoxically, stressful. Experienced meditators will recognize this. What happens when you sit still? First thing: your mind starts racing. More accurately, you notice how your mind is racing. That's called "monkey mind." When you're meditating, you're sitting still, and a still body helps still the mind. It eventually slows down and becomes more focused.

It's very common in forest bathing to find that at some point we've sped up and are walking at our ordinary hiking pace. That's because we lost focus, our minds started racing, and our body automatically kept up. We might call this "monkey body," as an outward expression of monkey mind. Because the mind and body are a single entity, slowing our body will also calm our mind.

The eternal movement of the forest gives our minds something to engage with. Just as with sitting meditation the breath is always there and available for watching, in the forest there are always things in motion. Your mind will drift, and many other thoughts will arise. When they do, gently bring your attention back to noticing what's in motion.

When you find you have automatically sped up, come to a complete halt for a moment. It's an opportunity to fully give your attention to one thing, noticing how that thing is in motion. After a brief pause you'll be ready to continue your slow walk.

I recommend that you walk like this for at least fifteen minutes. That's enough time for your mind to go through several cycles of distraction and calming. Many people notice that their inner calmness comes more easily and is stabler each time they come back to moving slowly and noticing what's in motion.

Notice what you are Noticing

After the invitation "Walking in Forest Time," take a few moments again to notice what you are noticing.

5. *Infinite Possibilities*

"Infinite Possibilities" is where, within the container of the optimal flow, forest bathers can choose from among infinite possibilities.

Invitations are everywhere in the forest. The grass invites us to lie in it. The clouds invite us to gaze. The hawk invites us to spread our arms like wings and walk as if we were flying. The steep part of the trail invites us to slow down and notice how we carry our center of gravity. The worm invites us to explore the dirt. These are simple invitations, easy to discover. With a group, you can turn this into a game, taking turns to offer your discovery to others: "I am the fallen tree. I invite you to walk on me."

"I am the singing stream. I invite you to find a way to add your music to mine." The possibilities are endless. Notice the format: the *noun* invites you to *verb*. This formula is called "the infinite invitation."

Eventually you will become adept at discovering what invitations the forest is offering to you. You'll learn to flow within the unique configuration of who you are, where you are in the forest, and when you are in the forest, with all the critters and elements and events unfolding within and around you.

The next chapter on invitations contains a sampling from among the hundreds that I and my fellow guides have tested. They are some of the "keepers," having proven to reliably support satisfying experiences. Try out those that appeal to you—and perhaps a couple that don't.

6. *Sit Spot*

Sit spot is a very simple and very powerful practice. It is one of the best methods of nature connection, supporting healing, cultivating awareness of self and others, and deepening relationships with the more-than-human world. When done in the context of forest bathing, sit spot is a practice-within-the-practice.

Although the preferred time for sit spot is toward the end of the walk, it is not an afterthought. When we do it at end of our forest bathing walks just before the tea ceremony, we are in a relaxed and attentive state of mind that is ideal for sit spot. This is not a formal meditation practice, and there are no expectations, other than to find a place that feels right and simply sit there. You may choose to journal, but writing may distract you from noticing many things that might otherwise make themselves known.

A very common sit spot experience is "the slow reveal." The longer you sit, the more you notice. You may sit for fifteen minutes before you realize tiny flowers are growing right in front of you. It may be twenty minutes before the shy fox pokes its nose out of a bush to get a better sniff of the human with the unusually still behavior. In the relative stillness, an inner stillness also emerges; when it does, the other beings in the area may respond by making themselves more readily known. A slow, patient sit is rewarded with new perceptions. It's not like you are looking for observations to capture, stalking them like a hunter. It's more like letting things reveal themselves when they choose.

Twenty minutes is a good minimum time for sit spot.

Besides sit spot during forest bathing, you can also find a place near your home that is convenient for you to visit easily and cultivate a regular sit spot practice there. It might be in your garden. Aim for at least three sit spot sessions of twenty minutes or more per week. Many forest bathers find that sit spot time is an ideal bridge between forest bathing experiences.

7. Tea Ceremony

An ideal way to begin the transition out of the forest bath is to brew a pot of tea to share with those who have been your companions on the walk. We call this the tea ceremony, but there is no formalized structure for it. It's not the same as the "Way of Tea" in Japan, nor does it try to replicate the social conventions of a traditional British high tea. It's just another enjoyable moment of forest bathing. Yet, all over the world, forest bathing guides delight in assembling tea sets and developing ceremonies that express their unique ways of forest bathing practice. I prefer to use a lightweight backpacking stove or thermos of hot water to make "trail tea" from herbs I have gathered along the path. Of course, if you don't know your local plants and aren't sure which ones are safe to use, you can bring along some tea in a thermos.

You may find it very rewarding to take a class from a local expert on herbal medicine. Eventually you may develop the self-confidence and knowledge to make trail tea safely.

Harvest plants in a respectful way. Overall, be guided by the ethic of tenderness. Let your heart lead you. Avoid unnecessary damage to plants when harvesting, and don't harvest plants that are not abundant.

Be mindful of regulations regarding harvesting plants; if it is not allowed because you are guiding in a state park or similar setting with prohibitions, either get specific permission from the land use managers or harvest elsewhere and bring the plants with you. If they are the same species as those found on the trail where you guide, they will be a good match.

In the off-season you can use plants that you gathered at other times and dried for winter use. Another option is to purchase plants at local herb stores. Again, find those species that grow along your trail.

Much of what makes an ordinary activity like drinking tea feel like a ceremony is the quality attention we give to it. Allow the tea ceremony to be a segue from the special circumstances of forest bathing back to normal, everyday life.

8. *The Threshold of Incorporation*

If you marked the Threshold of Connection to begin your walk, return to that place or choose a new place to cross a second threshold to formally end the walk. This second threshold is called the "Threshold of Incorporation." It begins during the tea ceremony, when you start transitioning from the liminal time of the forest bath back to ordinary activities like snacking and being in conversation. Just as you did at the beginning, a simple ceremony at the end is a clear demarcation when you can celebrate the end of your experience.

Pause at the threshold and consider the gifts you have received on your walk. Invite them into your deepest awareness, knowing that these gifts will be alive somewhere within you. This is what *incorporation* means: to take into the body, in-corpus. Step across the threshold, leaving liminality, and return to ordinary life, now carrying the gifts the forest has given.

• • •

Returning home, take care while you travel to be attentive and safe. Sometimes forest bathers are in a slightly altered, dreamlike state for an hour or so afterward. You may feel deeply relaxed and have a strong urge to nap. Just be aware of these tendencies and find ways to accommodate them safely.

5

THE FOREST INVITES YOU

The sampling of invitations here is arranged according to the ancient scheme of the four elements of earth, air, fire, and water. For most invitations I have also listed the senses predominantly involved.

Earth Invitations

We feel the earth rise up to support us each time we take a step. Our bodies are magnificently built to be held perfectly by the ground as we walk upright through gravity's embrace or lie in the meadow looking at clouds. Earth invitations cultivate our connection to the physical world where our lives unfold.

BAREFOOT WALKING (Touch)

The soles of our feet are rich with nerves that stimulate the entire body. Many health advocates hold that a half hour or so of barefoot walking should be a daily part of our health regimen. Recently proponents of "earthing" have advocated the idea that shoes insulate us from ground-flowing electrical currents that are essential for our well-being.

In good weather I often forest bathe in flip-flops. This allows me to easily go barefoot when the trail is smooth or sandy or mostly soft duff that is not too challenging for my feet. When I come to a rough patch, I can put my flip-flops back on. Sometimes I continue barefoot and practice slow, mindful walking. I notice that if I can keep my heart soft and not tense my body, even rough terrain can be crossed comfortably without shoes.

DIRT (Smell, Seeing, Touch, Taste)

What a wonderful substance dirt is, so vibrantly full of life! Sometimes when I pause with the group for a sharing circle I will notice a small pile of clean, freshly turned dirt made by a gopher (in your region, who are the animals that burrow and leave fresh piles of clean dirt?). Partnering with this little subterranean mammal for a moment, I will pick up a handful of dirt and use it as a talking piece. It is full of aroma and texture, and the surprise of passing it from hand to hand brings a moment of levity. After it has been passed around, everyone's hands are a bit dirty. I invite us to smell the scent of dirt on our hands. When we do, what memories appear in our bodies and minds? For me, the smell of dirt recalls my grandfather's hands, working the soil of his abundant garden. This is a memory of considerable emotional power, connecting me across the years with the sensuality of childhood wonder.

Return your handful to the forest floor, then taste the traces left on your fingers. Studies have shown that we are more disease-resistant when our diets include traces of dirt (provided, of course, that it is of healthy soil, not polluted with human-made toxins).

The duff on the forest floor—that rich mix of decomposing leaves, grasses, and fungi—has more texture than simple dirt, and a handful of duff will likely have several tiny critters in it. You can pick up a handful and explore it with sight and touch and smell; taste it if you are adventurous enough. Notice what you are noticing.

Considering what you have received, what can you give back to the dirt?

THE FOREST FLOOR (Smell, Seeing, Touch)

Explore a portion of the forest floor on your hands and knees. You might bring along a magnifying glass for this. Take your time. Notice what you are noticing. This is a great rainy-day invitation if you are prepared with waterproof pants and coat.

FEELING ANIMAL TRACKS (Seeing, Body Radar)

Animal tracks often appear on the forest floor. When you come across a set of deer prints, or perhaps raccoon prints along a creek, or the winding line on a dusty trail where a snake has traveled, pause and look closely. Put your hand on a portion of the track, such as the imprint of a deer hoof. Can you feel some trace of the animal's presence? Speaking out loud, describe the sensations or impressions you are getting. After developing a connection with the tracks in this way, close your eyes while still staying in contact with the track. Relax and let your intuition feel the animal's current location. Eyes still closed, point in the direction that your body senses. If you are doing this in a group, when everyone is pointing, open your eyes together and compare notes. What are you noticing?

THE JOY OF TINY THINGS (Seeing, Heart Sense, Body Radar)

As you wander, notice small things on the ground. Which of them are appealing to you? Gather a dozen or so. Then find a place where you can arrange them. Let the arrangement emerge naturally. Then wander and find more items, and return and add them also. If you are doing this in a group, each person can create their own, or you can create one together. What are you noticing?

CALL ON THE WOOD-WIDE WEB (Imaginal)

This invitation is done with a flower or any rooted thing. Suggest that the roots of the plant are tightly connected to the ancient and most powerful internet, a global system of communication linking all plants and soil organisms to the earth. You can speak into the flower to "telephone" the earth. Have a phone conversation with it, beginning with a greeting. Be sure to give plenty of time to listen for her responses. Let your imagination guide you. After this invitation, people can share in pairs. This is a great invitation for Mother's Day; you can have a nice conversation with "mother earth," including a picnic with her!

GRAVITY (Proprioception)

This is an invitation I learned while I was in Japan. On a gentle slope, put out a piece of fabric large enough to lie down on. The fabric the Japanese guide used was slightly slippery. Lie facing up, but with your head downhill. Experience the gentle pull of gravity; let yourself slowly slide down the hill. Do this for about two minutes.

FIND A STONE ALLY (Imaginal)

Who among us has not collected stones? I rarely meet anyone who does not have a special stone in their home or garden, perhaps one that they have brought back from a distant land. Stones have made long journeys over eons of time, some of them spanning multiple continents. They have been continually reshaped, bathed in fire, held deep in the embrace of the earth, and inspected by the light of the sun, moon, and stars. A few have traveled from other planets. There are an infinite number of stones on this planet, yet each one is unique. In some traditions, stones are believed to possess their own spirits.

For the stone invitations, you need to find a place where there is a good selection of stones that range in size from golf ball to grapefruit. The edges of streams are often ideal.

Wander and see what stone calls to you. If there are hazards such as the possibility of scorpions or a venomous snake under the stones, pick the stone up carefully to ensure it is critter-free. Simply finding a stone is an invitation in itself. You can pause here and notice what you are noticing.

You could also continue with one or more of the following stone invitations, which make up a subcategory of the earth invitations. Some of them can be done individually; some require working in pairs.

HOLDING THE STONE (Seeing, Touch, Smell, Proprioception, Imaginal)

Hold the stone. Explore it visually. Then, eyes closed, continue your exploration with touch. Notice the ways in which it is unique. Imagine the journey your stone has been through to bring it to this moment. How many years, eons, epochs have elapsed? What has happened with the landscape and the climate? How deep in the earth, how immersed in waters has this stone been? Perhaps it carries a long story, if only we know how to listen. Perhaps it has accumulated wisdom, and patience, and the capacity to hold and endure a great deal of pressure and release.

EXPERIENCING EMBODIMENT WITH STONES
(Proprioception, Body Radar, Heart Sense)

Eyes closed, hold the stone with both hands, close to your heart. Feel the presence of the stone. Now, holding it with only one hand, slowly move it away from your chest out in front of you. Notice any sensations you experience in your body. How does the weight of the stone make itself known throughout your body?

Eyes still closed, slowly move the stone around, from side to side, up and down, in circles, continually noticing the sensations in your body. See if there are places along the arcs of movement where your body just feels right.

Eyes still closed, try curling your toes into the earth and see if that changes how you experience the stone. Curl them up and see what happens.

Eyes still closed, instead of moving the stone, in a relaxed way allow it to guide you. Where does it want to go? How does it want to be moved? Like a dancer, follow the stone's lead.

Eyes still closed, bring the stone back to your heart, holding it with both hands. Feel its presence.

In a moment—but not yet—you will open your eyes and see the stone again, perhaps in a new way. Hold the stone in front of you with both hands. Now, open your eyes. Take a few moments to explore the stone with your eyes and hands.

ASK A STONE FOR SUPPORT (Imaginal, Heart Sense)

People sometimes come to forest bathing carrying a full load of preoccupations, worries, and mental distractions. This is just our normal way of being; we have monkey mind. Being in the forest, our minds begin to slow down naturally. However, there may be persistent worries that can distract us during the walk. A stone ally can serve as a "worry stone," and this is a very effective way to call on the support of the more-than-human world. It is a form of partnership with nature that can help us to stay present and embodied.

Hold your stone to your heart and either mentally or in a whisper ask the stone if it will hold your worry while you forest bathe, so you don't have to carry the worry with you. Probably whatever you are worrying about, you worry about for a reason; just know that your stone will let you pick up your worry again after the walk if you choose to, although by that time you may have a different perspective about your worry and it might feel as if it has changed.

When you are ready, place your stone somewhere you can find it later. If you would like, you can share out loud what you have asked the stone to hold, or you may prefer to keep it just between you and the stone people.

INTRODUCING YOUR STONE (Heart Sense, Imaginal)

This invitation is done in pairs.

Introduce your stone to another person in the circle. Share about your experience with your stone with your partner. Next, exchange stones. What is it like to hold a different stone? What is it like to hold a stone that has supported another person's journey? Allow your heart and your stone to guide you in how to bring your interaction to a close.

Air Invitations

There is a scene in the 2006 film *Fearless*, starring Jet Li, where Li's character is under the care of villagers in a remote region of China while he is healing from emotional and physical trauma. He is working with them in a rice paddy, close to the earth, ankle-deep in water, under the heat of the sun. Through the air comes the sound of the bamboo forest on the hillside rattling in a gust of wind. The villagers set down their tools, turn and face the forest, and spread their arms to embrace the wind. It is a powerful moment. The relationship between the people and the sky is palpable; they know the wind, like the water and the rice and the sun, is essential, that it is the breath of life. It is a moment of humble, simple celebration. It is tending a relationship.

This is the air element. Anything that has to do with breathing, smelling, and noticing what is in motion involves the element of air. There are many possibilities. Here are some ideas.

FOREST BREATHING (Proprioception, Smell, Taste)

Every guided forest bathing experience I had in Japan included *shinrin kokyu*, or "forest breathing." Our breath is so important, and many of us are habitually shallow breathers. Our blood is therefore not completely oxygenated. Deep breathing has long been part of many health practices. In the forest, the benefits are amplified because the air has a higher proportion of fresh, clean oxygen, direct from the trees. There are also beneficial phytoncides in the air. In some places, like near a waterfall, the air is full of negative ions, which have positive effects on our bodies.

Each guide taught deep breathing differently from the others, but the general principle was the same. Here's an example: Breathe in slowly for eight seconds, fully expanding your diaphragm and pushing the belly out. Hold the breath for five seconds. Then slowly exhale for ten seconds. Repeat at least five times. Our guides recommended doing ten to twenty cycles of shinrin kokyu, twice a day.

The forest breathing invitations were usually given in the middle portion of the walk. I noticed that I felt refreshed and invigorated afterward, with more energy for the rest of the walk.

ACHIEVE NOTHING (No Senses, All Senses)

Try this for a portion of your walk: Let go of achieving anything. Allow yourself no goals, nothing to do, nothing to reach. Don't even try to achieve not-achieving. Don't try to not do; just not do. Notice what you are noticing.

RECIPROCITY BREATHING (Imaginal, Heart Sense)

Breathing in, be aware of what you are receiving from the trees. Breathing out, be aware of what you are returning. Breathing deeply, receive the gifts of the forest in your entire body. Breathing out, return the essence of your gift. Notice what you are noticing.

CLOUD WATCHING (Seeing, Mirror, Imaginal)

Remember watching clouds as a child, seeing the shapes of fantastic creatures appear and then morph slowly into something new? I wonder how many adults have in their minds that they will do this again, someday, when they are not too busy? On a forest therapy walk, you can easily reexperience this simple joy. If the clouds and the weather are right, find a good place to lie down and simply gaze. Don't be too grown-up and serious; let the child's mind take over. Let the images and the feelings they stir flow.

SWAYING (Proprioception, Body Radar, Imaginal, Mirror)

This is a good invitation for a meadow area surrounded by trees, or anyplace where trees can be seen in their entirety from at least ten yards' distance. A day with a steady breeze is best for this; bear in mind that a breeze may not be as apparent to people on the ground as it is to trees with their crowns higher in the sky.

See what tree is inviting you to gaze at it. Facing the tree, let your own roots sink into the ground. Flexible like the limbs of the tree, sway with the tree. How do the trees feel the wind? As their limbs flex, do they sense the wind as a flowing force in their bodies or how sap is flowing within them? As you sway, can you feel the wind moving within you also? Is there a relationship in your body between wind and bone, wind and blood? If you change the way you are swaying, can you feel changes in how the wind flows through you? Are you separate from the wind? Notice what you are noticing.

SCENT TRACKING (Smell)

Wander until you notice a scent, then follow it as far as your nose will take you. It may fade after only a few steps, but over time you'll find your sense of smell sharpening and you'll track scents farther.

When you lose the scent, pause and see if it comes back to you. Bear in mind that scents change subtly, so while you are tracking, don't just follow a static scent, but sense how it changes. When you are done with one scent, you can wander until you find another. Allow ten to fifteen minutes for this. If you are with others, go out in pairs to show each other what your noses have noticed and to see if your partner can pick up the same scent. Partners can try to follow each other's scent trails and see if their paths are the same.

SOUND TRACKING (Hearing)

Choose a place where natural sounds are predominant and not submerged under human-made sounds, when there is a steady stream of sounds from insects, birds, water, and breezes. Standing still, listen to the soundscape. Choose one sound and wander toward it. You may arrive at its source; greet it with a sound of your own. Or it may fade away. Pause, choose another sound, and follow it.

You can also enter a conversation with any sound in the forest, by making sounds or speaking words out loud, as you approach the source of the sound. Approach slowly, quietly, allowing it to become accustomed to your presence, listening as you do.

MOVING THROUGH THE SKY (Imaginal, Proprioception)

This is a wandering invitation. Invite people to be aware that, above the soles of their feet, their bodies inhabit the lowest layer of sky. For a few moments, move with this in your awareness. What is it like to move from one place in the sky to another? Are there any differences from one piece of sky to the next? Notice what you are noticing.

EMBRACE THE WIND (Heart Sense, Proprioception, Touch, Hearing, Seeing)

Remember that scene I described earlier from the film *Fearless*? As in the movie, sometimes when we are in the forest, zephyrs of wind will pass through. We hear them moving toward us before their touch reaches the trees around us. Simply turn toward the wind and spread your arms in an embrace. If it is a day when there are several zephyrs, this may become part of the practice of the day. Notice what you are noticing.

GREEN MANSIONS (Imaginal, Heart Sense, Seeing, Hearing, Smell, Touch)

When I was in my teens and early twenties, I took many journeys into the backcountry of the Los Padres National Forest, over the ridge of the Santa Ynez Mountains that rose behind my hometown of Santa Barbara. I loved walking up the twisting canyon trails. Each time I came around a bend, there was a distinctly new part of the canyon, with its own unique feel, like a room in a mansion has its own style. And, just up ahead, another bend in the canyon would entice me to move forward and discover a new "sense room." Each discovery was a delight; it was this experience of the unique sensory signature of each place that kept me coming back time and again, exploring one trail after another, mile upon mile of delight.

Noticing the unique feel of places is a part of coming into relationship with them. The impressions we receive from the energetic signature of a place are part of what we call the "felt sense of the present moment." Felt mainly in the regions of our hearts and bellies, it is a delicious noticing. Every place offers us its own self; and the self of a place is a mirror into our own selves. Green Mansions explore this on a smaller, but just as potent, scale than a whole section of canyon. It is one of the invitations that, when properly delivered, invites child's mind to come out and play.

Begin by walking slowly along the trail, noticing when you cross invisible boundaries between one experience of the trail and the next. For example, you might come around a corner where suddenly the sounds of a nearby stream leap vividly forward. This sensory experience defines a new "room" or section of the trail. Place a stone or other marker at the place where this change occurred. Then continue along the trail until you again sense that the trail is passing through yet another room. Usually this happens every twenty to thirty feet or so. Mark three to five transition points. Now, backtrack. This will help you tune in to the felt sense of place.

What senses are involved in recognizing the unique presence of each place? Find a way to describe what is unique about each room along the trail. One way to do this is to give it a name. Often these will be whimsical names, such as "the Fairy Dance-a-Torium." Or they may be more prosaic like, "the Reading Room." What are the felt characteristics of this place? Where is the furniture in the room? Perhaps a fallen log is a couch, a stone is a tea table, a cluster of flowers is the "scent stove." Where are the windows? How about the door; is there a best place to enter and leave this room?

Next, if the forest allows it, wander off-trail until you find a room that feels right to you. You may try several rooms before you settle on one; that may take up to ten minutes. You'll sense where the walls are. Then enjoy and explore it for fifteen or twenty minutes. Use your imagination to see it as a child would. Let it reveal its name to you.

If you are walking with a group, you can give tours to each other of your rooms in the forest's green mansion. I know when groups are doing this, because the woods fill with childlike laughter.

Notice what you are noticing: Has discovering your own room affected your sense of relationship to this forest? How? Was there anything your sense room offered you that seems to speak to something about your life as it is now?

Water Invitations

Water is a fundamental requirement for all life, a source of great beauty and healing. Water carries the essence of love and peace. Include interactions with water on every walk, if possible.

There are a great many possible ways to come into sensory contact with water. Choose a few of them, being sensitive to your needs and those of others. Some possibilities are listed here, roughly in order from least to most edgy. The edgiest ones, such as those involving water blessings, are often the most powerful, but their power may not be welcome. Let your intuition guide you.

Whenever possible, choose a trail from which a running wild stream can be easily accessed. Avoid any place where access requires a descent down a steep, trailless bank or through brambles or nettles or over loose rocks.

As with all things about forest bathing, aim to make it ease-full.

Ponds or lakes will serve, as will rivers, so long as they can be interacted with easily and safely. The best option is a smallish stream that runs year-round, is clear and clean, and remains free of upstream polluters like agricultural chemicals or livestock grazing.

In much of the world it's almost impossible to find a stream with water that we can safely drink anymore, but we can find water that smells good, runs clear, and can be safely touched, poured on our bodies, and waded in. It is also possible to find places to swim, but swimming is not typically included in a forest bathing walk.

A small stream running through gentle terrain provides a soundscape that is more conducive to forest bathing than does a larger stream making rambunctious happy noises over cascades and rapids. The quiet gurgle of a brook is relaxing and has the advantage of not competing with the voice of the guide who is giving invitations to the group.

You should be able to easily touch the water. Ideally, you can sit and remove your shoes to immerse your feet. When I am guiding a group, I will sometimes do a bit of streambank-tending, to clear away driftwood or other impediments that might make it difficult for the group to spread out at the water's edge, always with close attention to the aesthetics of the place and maintaining its natural appearance. Where no streams or natural bodies of water are available, it is possible to work with fountains or garden ponds, albeit in a more limited way.

Often where you find water, you also find mosquitoes. If you live in territory where there are many mosquitoes, another thing to look for is a place that is open to local breezes, which can help to minimize their presence.

SIT SPOT BY WATER (Imaginal, Hearing, Seeing, Smell)

The simplest water invitation is to find a sit spot along the stream. This form of interacting with water often creates a dreamlike meditative state. Settle for a while, long enough for the "slow reveal" to unfold. Twenty minutes is about right. Notice what you are noticing.

GAZING AT WATER (Seeing, Heart Sense, Body Radar)

Gazing at water is another simple invitation. As with gazing at a tree or a mountain, it is helpful to set a goal of five to eight minutes and use a watch to stick to it. Remember that in forest bathing, gazing is done not just with the eyes, but with the whole body and all the senses. Notice what you are noticing.

WATERFALLS (Proprioception, Seeing, Smell, Taste, Touch)

Near a small waterfall a gentle mist flows in the air. A long tradition exists in Japan of women sitting in the air below waterfalls. They are taking advantage of the beneficial effects of the negative ions in the air on their complexions. Forest bathing not only makes us healthier, it can also make us even better-looking than we already are (if such a thing were possible!).

TOUCHING WATER (Touch, Heart Sense)

Touching water provides many sensory and sensual possibilities. Find a place where you can comfortably and safely sit or crouch down at the edge of a shallow stream or pond. Touch the water as lightly as possible. Gently stroke the surface of the water. Next rest your palm on the surface of the stream and slowly push it down, noticing the texture of the water and what sensations you experience in your hand

and elsewhere in your body as you push slowly deeper, and then as you slowly lift your hand out of the water. What is it like to move your hand through the forest air while it is covered with water? What other playful experiments can you discover? Notice what you are noticing.

FEET IN THE STREAM (Touch, Heart Sense)

Removing your shoes and putting your feet in the water are simple things, and on a hot day, can be a wonderful, sensual relief. I like to take flip-flops on my forest bathing walks and wade where the stream is shallow, keeping to a slow shinrin-yoku pace. A trekking pole or walking stick can be helpful for balance if the stream has a rocky bottom. Do this for as long as you enjoy it. Notice what you are noticing.

A FOREST BATH IN THE WATER (Touch, Seeing, Hearing, Body Radar)

Recently I was walking in a shallow stream, where the water rarely rose above the middle of my calf. It was a very hot day, a record-breaker. I was wearing my flip-flops and hiking shorts made of a fast-drying fabric. There was a deeper place, a tiny pond where I could sit with the water coming to mid-chest. The water was cool, not cold. Thirty minutes sitting in that tiny pond was a wonderful forest bath and a perfect sit spot!

You don't need a big swimming hole; even a small, shallow pond is sufficient. On cooler days, in colder water, a quick in-and-out dip will invigorate your entire body. Try it! Notice what you are noticing.

MUD SQUISH (Touch)

Some streams offer the opportunity to squish mud through your toes. Playing with mud is sometimes the natural thing to do; you can use it to paint your body and face (and your companion's as well). On one of the guided forest bathing walks I experienced in Japan, the guides led us up a shallow concrete flume with rushing cold water. At the top we stepped out into a spot of muddy dirt. After the stream, the mud felt warm. Mud is inherently sensual; you can't really just feel it physically without also having an emotional experience. Our group lingered with our feet in the mud for several minutes, then some of us waded back down through the cold water, while others chose the trail.

The guides thoughtfully supplied small towels for cleaning and drying our feet.

In a Canadian forest, a woman who was using the "Green Mansions" invitation to explore sense rooms found one in a muddy bank at the edge of a stream. She called over the other forest bathers in the group, who joined her one by one until we were all there. Each of us was "initiated" into her sense room by having our faces painted in its mud. Forest bathing meets body art.

In the mud, notice what you are noticing.

WATER MUSIC (Hearing, Heart Sense, Proprioception)

Water is inherently musical. Join in the music of the stream by splashing, striking rocks together rhythmically, and experimenting with other ways to make sound. Use your voice to explore making sounds that weave together with those of the water. Notice what you are noticing.

WATER MESSENGER (Imaginal)

You can ask water to carry messages. What would you like the world to know? What is something that you would like to say to another person, but don't know how?

What is one thing you hope you will remember, but worry you might forget? You can ask water to hold and carry your thoughts. Use your cupped hands to scoop up some water. Bring it close to your lips, then whisper your message. Release the water back into the stream.

Consider some of the ways the water might carry and disseminate your message. One of my ANFT colleagues tells a story of a group of corporate clients who sent messages in a stream. An hour later there was a brief rainstorm. They were ecstatic to receive their messages back from the rain! Notice what you are noticing.

ASK THE WATER A QUESTION (Imaginal)

A variation of the previous invitation is to ask the water a personal question, perhaps having to do with a challenge or dilemma for which you seek clarity. This works best when your walk crosses a stream twice, with the first crossing upstream from the second. At the first crossing, whisper your question into the water. Later, when you are crossing again downstream, sit quietly along the stream bank. The water has tumbled your question about—which is one of water's ways of thinking things over—and may have something to offer you, if you listen closely. Notice what you are noticing.

WATER BLESSING (Imaginal, Heart Sense)

One sensuous, simple act is to bathe your hands. Scoop water with one hand and pour it slowly over the other, giving full attention to the sensations. As you do, let it be a time to honor your hands for all the many ways in which they have served you. Bless your hands, offering gratitude and encouragement for their long and faithful service.

Bathing the hands easily segues into pouring water over your head. Let doing so be an expression of tenderness and support for all of who you are.

If you are with a companion, consider bathing each other's hands or feet. This is a very intimate action, and it requires full permission and the right kind of flow in the moment and in your relationship. Even more intimate, and simultaneously more playful, is pouring water on each other's heads.

When pouring water on another person, it is possible to offer them a blessing: "May you be well," for example, or "may these hands continue to give you joy." One of the natural partnerships between people and water is that people have the power to give blessings, and water has the power to carry those blessings. This knowledge is encoded in religious traditions such as baptism. Because of its religious associations, some people will feel receiving water blessings from others is not for them. It's important to be sensitive to and respect this.

Notice what you are noticing.

RECIPROCITY INVITATIONS FOR WATER (Heart Sense, Imaginal)

After using some of the invitations above (or others of your own), explore what can you offer to the water. I often sing to it:

> O, water, sweet water
> Let me tell you how I am feeling
> You have given me such pleasure
> I love you so.

When I sing, the waters of my blood and spirit are quickened with love and gratitude for all the waters of the world and the forests that filter and cleanse them.

Fire Invitations

Fire symbolizes the energy of relationships. The invitations in this section are primarily about igniting and tending the fire of relationships with the more-than-human world rather than working with actual flames.

SPEAK OUT LOUD (Imaginal)

As with many forest bathing invitations, this one has two parts. One part is receiving; the other is practicing reciprocity by giving. When these parts are practiced together, we may discover levels of communication that were previously beyond what we thought possible.

The first part of the invitation is to receive the sights, sounds, and sensations the forest offers as communication from it to you and to the other beings of the forest.

Imagine that each sound you hear and motion you see is *purposeful*—for example, the movement of branches in the wind. Our social conditioning leads us to automatically assume that these sounds are random and meaningless, resulting from essentially mechanical forces, such as wind pushing branches on which the leaves rustle. Mostly, we simply screen these sounds out. On our forest baths, let's allow for the story that all sounds are the forest talking and we are included in the conversation.

We may make similar assumptions about the various voices of birds, thinking they are meaningless. They are, after all, just "bird sounds." To a birder, perhaps they are useful for identifying what species are present. But most people don't see them as meaningful beyond that. With just a bit of observation, however, we quickly learn that birds are constantly talking purposefully among themselves. In his brilliant study of bird language *What the Robin Knows*, naturalist and master tracker Jon Young unpacks the depth and sophistication of bird language, both "spoken" and inherent in their behaviors, what we might call "body language."

I've learned from Jon how, when I'm sitting in my garden reading, to tell exactly where my cat is, based on the warnings the towhees are giving each other and the behaviors of the smaller songbirds. This is a basic level of listening to nature. Tracking the movement of your cat by listening to and observing birds is low-hanging fruit for learning bird language. It opens the door just a crack, through which you can peer into a vast world of expanded possibility for connection, one that you can cultivate for a lifetime. I am often aware when the birds are talking about me. And the birds are just one section of the forest's infinite orchestra.

The second part of the invitation is to communicate back. Speak to the forest out loud. Greet the many beings you notice by name: Hello, trail. Hello, willow. Hello, creek. Hello, my two feet standing. Hello, stones. Hello, you old married raven couple who so often appear when I walk. Like the sounds of the stream, the wind in the trees, and the songs of the breeze and insects, your voice belongs here. Claim that belonging. Notice how speaking helps you arrive. Movements and gesture are also ways we speak to the forest. Just let your body flow; you may find yourself dancing ecstatically. Try this on a rainy day with the storm as your partner. Doing this, I feel I am "loving out loud."

It may strike you as a bit silly the first time you try this invitation, but it's very powerful. The first time I tried it, I discovered that talking out loud and making gestures helped me notice each tree, stone, and turn in the trail more vividly than before. When I returned to the same place again, weeks later, I noticed a change. I felt much more connected to that section of trail. And it seemed to me that the trees and plants there were more awake and attentive and, perhaps, happier to see me than before our speaking-out-loud encounter.

CONVERSATION WITH A TREE (Imaginal)

Trees are very patient listeners. They are nonjudgmental; you can tell them anything, without fearing they will lose their respect for you, or turn your secrets into malicious gossip. They don't bill by the hour, and they're willing to give you as much time as you need. You can say a quick hello as you pass by, or you can sit next to, lean against, climb into the branches of, or lie beneath one for hours. You don't have to say anything at all; trees have a presence that is naturally relaxing.

People who talk with trees often feel that what they receive in return is wisdom. An old oak that I knew well fell in a winter storm. I sat on its trunk, near its massive root-ball, and told it of my sorrow at its passing. As is typical in moments of imaginal sensing, *there came over me a knowing* that the tree experienced the event of its fall very differently from what I had assumed. It told me, "My falling is a threshold in a ceremony of fulfillment of my life. For the next few years I will continue to provide shelter for many other beings, while I also build the soil and prepare it to carry life forward. That life will be an expression of what I have been, just as I have been a continuity of the trees that came before me." At my age, this teaching resonates powerfully with me. I've had many similar teachings from trees, as have those I have guided.

"Conversation with a Tree" invites you to both speak and listen. When speaking, there are many topics you can explore. For example:

- Ask the tree a question about your life, health, or relationships.

- Tell the tree something that you've never been able to speak about with another person.

- Give the tree compliments; notice out loud its many gifts.

- Share your sorrow.

- Ask the tree for advice.

- Ask the tree to support you on your forest bathing walk. Tell it what you need help with.

As with any conversation, good manners are important. If you and the tree are new to each other, introduce yourself. Get to know the tree a little bit. Trees don't rush about, and you will become more attuned to the tree when you take your time and approach it attentively, without hurrying. The next invitation, "Gazing," helps with the attunement process.

GAZING (Mirror, Body Radar, Imaginal, Heart Sense, Seeing)

Before approaching a tree, I will often stand at a distance where I can gaze at it with a kind of whole-body attention that involves not just seeing, but also feeling the tree. To restrain any tendency to rush, I use my watch and time this period of gazing so it lasts a full five minutes. Often, after several minutes I strongly feel that the tree is gazing back at me. It is then that I feel the time is right to approach it.

Trees like to be touched and appreciated. They respond well to thoughtful pruning. When a relationship between a person and a tree develops over time, the person will often experience a special bond with the tree, and many memorable events and learnings will accumulate. If the person actively tends the tree, there will likely be evidence of the tree also experiencing this bond. It may take on a beautiful shape. A young tree may grow more quickly; an older tree may seem to hold its place with more dignity. The ecosystem that forms around trees thus tended will become more robust with birds and squirrels, mosses, and other beings. This ecosystem includes humans. When you form a relationship with a tree, you become part of its ecosystem. It also becomes part of your ecosystem. Its roots begin to reach into your imagination, and its branches become spiritual shelter.

It is good to meet many trees and to treat all with courtesy and respect. It is also important to find those that invite you into an ongoing relationship with them. Often these are the trees near where you live. You may have had the habit of taking them for granted or of thinking of them in limited ways—as decoration, for example. They invite you into a more conscious awareness of their personhood.

Speaking to trees is rewarding; it can help us shape our thoughts, give voice to questions, and calm and soothe our worries. But listening to trees is even more rewarding. When we ask a tree a question, we can learn to listen for an answer. Even people who are very skeptical and strongly committed to the scientific, rational view that trees are insentient vegetables will often have interesting experiences, sometimes challenging what they think they know, when they listen to trees. They often come away feeling wiser.

OFFERING FRIENDSHIP (Imaginal, Body Radar)

This is a very simple invitation. Find a tree and offer your friendship to it and the forest. Think about how you would do this with a person, or a cat, or a dog. How much would you speak, and how much would you listen? What would be your opening conversational gambits, your first flirtation?

In an area where there are at least several approachable trees, feel the one your body radar is guiding you toward. Consider the story that all trees are connected, so when you speak with that tree, assume the whole forest is listening in like nosy but benevolent relatives. The forest may be giving the tree advice about how to communicate back and what to "say." Notice what you are noticing.

OF LIFE'S JOURNEY (Heart Sense)

"Of Life's Journey" is a wandering invitation. It helps to cultivate a felt sense of the present moment and often supports finding a deeper sense of acceptance and gratitude for even the difficult circumstances of one's life.

While walking slowly through the forest, as you notice various features, incorporate them into this sentence, speaking out loud:

"The _____ of life's journey."

For example:

"The rough bark of life's journey."

"The flowing water of life's journey."

"The dusty trail of life's journey."

"The broken branch of life's journey."

"The tangled roots of life's journey."

"The spiral shape of life's journey."

Don't go beyond simply saying the sentences. Try not make any intellectual effort; do not slip into discursive analysis or trying to discover what the metaphor means. Simply let each sentence land in your heart, then move to the next.

I recommend ten minutes of "Of Life's Journey" wandering.

Notice what you are noticing.

THREADS OF CONNECTION (Body Radar, Heart Sense, Imaginal)

This invitation is also sometimes called "Bungee Bow," because bowing is a gesture that is often made to express respect and greeting. In Zen, it is called *gassho*, referring to a bow with hands held in front, palms touching, signifying respect and attentiveness. Bowing feels good; it gentles the heart.

When we first connect with another being, a thread-like energy comes into being. It connects to our hearts or bellies or sometimes our solar plexus. If we tend to this nascent energetic connection, it grows stronger. The thread becomes a string; the string becomes a rope.

These ropes are infinitely elastic. Think of someone you love, or perhaps a companion animal in your life, with whom you have a strong, well-developed connecting rope. When you travel, even on the other side of world, even if you are apart for months, the rope is there; it grows as long as it needs to be. It exerts a tug, like a gentle bungee cord, pulling you back toward each other. Threads of Connection is an invitation to notice and cultivate these ropes.

Use your body radar to see if you feel a tug like a bungee cord pulling you in a certain direction. You don't have to have any idea regarding what is tugging you. Just notice it and let it pull you. Wander in that direction, trusting the tugging to guide you. You'll know the source of the tug when you see it, so long as you don't overthink it. When you arrive, explore the sensations of the connection. Introduce yourself. Perhaps have a dialogue with the being; explore what kind of relationship you both agree would be desirable.

Perhaps you will have a sense of the bungee thickening into a stronger bond.

When you feel complete, make a gesture to the being. Before you turn away, indicate your farewell to it with a bow or whatever other gesture feels natural.

After bowing, slowly turn with palms facing forward and let your body radar sense another tug. Follow it. Each encounter may be unique; let each conversation, the felt connection, and the gesture that appears stand on its own. Honor your intuition.

This can be repeated three or four times, or for as long as you like. It could be the main focus of one of your forest baths. I suspect it could develop into the core of a whole new practice. Notice what you are noticing.

A SECRET FOREST PLACE CALLING (Imaginal, Body Radar)

This is like "Threads of Connection" at a distance. In this invitation we use our imagination to contact some part of the forest that we may never actually visit. Perhaps it is a place that is aware you are visiting and would like to support you or to just make its presence known. It may be a place that exists in the physical world or only in the potent landscape of imagination. It may even straddle those two worlds, belonging to neither and both.

With your eyes closed, place your feet slightly apart and take up a solid stance. Imagine that rootlets are growing down from your feet into the earth. Picture them exploring as they grow, encountering fungi, subsoil critters, stones, roots of other beings, hidden waterways. Spread your roots horizontally so they reach far into the forest. You may notice these rootlets have a preferred direction; let them guide you on your imaginal journey.

In the forest the roots of many things are tangled and spreading. In your mind's eye, imagine that a place or being is reaching out to you with its own roots. Let your roots greet each other. Now, send your imagination along the roots that you have befriended until you come to their source. What is the place like? Let images and impressions form fully in your mind, like a scene in a film.

When your sense of this place is fully formed, decide how you want to continue your new friendship. Have a conversation with something you meet there and come to an understanding. Then, saying goodbye for now, come back to your own roots, and pull them back toward you through the forest floor, bringing them home to your feet. With your roots completely withdrawn, move your feet and come back to the place you are standing. Notice what you are noticing.

LET YOUR SOFT HEART GUIDE YOU (Heart Sense)

Exposure to chronic stress hardens the emotional quality of our hearts, and it also damages the heart physically. By feeling into our hearts, we can sense when we are feeling more hard-hearted and when we are feeling more softhearted.

Softheartedness—an open, expansive, feeling of gentleness toward oneself and others—is a state worthy of cultivation. With practice, anyone can learn to find their soft heart in any situation. When we allow our soft hearts to guide us, we make choices that are kinder. We can listen more openly to the voices of others. And we can consider a wider range of options when we are making decisions. The soft heart is intelligent and wise; it can be trusted. The forest is an ideal place to nurture our softheartedness.

This invitation is a way to cultivate our awareness of our soft heart and practice letting it guide us.

Pause and take a few deep breaths. Notice where you are. Feel into your heart region. What you encounter there may be a complex constellation of feelings. Find the seat of your softheartedness. Breathe into it; become attuned to your soft heart.

Now, begin to wander, either staying on the trail or, if the situation allows, moving into the forest or perhaps a meadow. Inwardly ask your soft heart to guide you. What will happen can't be predicted; each person discovers their own way of doing it and makes their own meaning of it.

6

LEANING INTO THE LEARNING EDGES

Our worlds are bounded by what we know. Each time we learn something new, the edges of our world expand. When we lean into a challenging situation, we enlarge our sense of possibility and our range of knowledge, and our world expands. Forest bathing presents learning edges for many of its practitioners. Some edges are easy. Some are challenging. Here we'll review some of the most common.

Beginner's Mind

If you already have a great deal of experience of nature, an edge for you may be letting go of being an expert. Try to approach forest bathing with "beginner's mind." This beautiful term was introduced by Japanese Zen master

Shunryu Suzuki, who played a major role in introducing Zen to the West. His book *Zen Mind, Beginner's Mind* opens with this simple statement:

> In the beginner's mind there are many possibilities;
> But in the expert's there are few.[5]

This is a good guideline for forest bathing. If you are used to being an authority, it may be stressful for you to be a beginner. But just as becoming an authority expanded your world, letting go of your certainty will create openings for it to expand even more.

Let the Forest Be Your Guide

You may be familiar with the study that says time in nature can produce a feeling of awe. That's great, but facts like this can also be a trap. You might then believe that when you go into the forest it's important to feel awe. Next thing you know, you are trying to create that feeling. But when you are trying for a specific outcome, it's more difficult for authentic feelings to emerge. And if you don't achieve your expected outcome, you may conclude that you've failed or that forest bathing has failed.

A more helpful perspective is to go in without expectations. The story I tell myself and offer to those I guide is that *the forest will decide for each one of us what experience we need.* No two of us will have the same experience. One may indeed feel awe, but another may be immersed in sorrow. Yet another may feel an urge to nap. Trust that the forest will guide you to what will speak to you. There is no need to make forest bathing into a precious, spiritual experience. Trying to make it "Zen" will prevent it from being so. Just relax and lean in to what is given.

No, You're Not Wasting Time

When we slow down, we may find an altered sense of time challenges us in a new way. It is not unusual to feel impatient or bored. We encounter what physician Larry Dossey calls "time sickness":

> Victims of time sickness are obsessed with the notion that time is getting away, that there isn't enough of it. . . . The trouble is, the body has

limits that it imposes on us. . . . If we try to beat it into submission and ask more of it than it can deliver . . ., it will let us know. The typical signals the body sends are migraine headaches, irritable bowels, sleep disorders and low-grade depression. . . . *What sets time-sick people apart is that when stressful conditions are removed, they continue to race the clock. They find it agonizing to wait,* because waiting means that precious seconds are slipping away. Stuck in line or waiting for a bus, they can't stop glancing at their watches. . . .[6] (italics mine)

Many times I've been moving slowly through the forest when the unbidden thought appears: "Isn't there something more important I should be doing?" With this thought comes a wave of anxiety, and I'm likely to automatically start walking faster. The way past this is to be aware of the thought when it occurs and to see it as a story, not a fact. We don't have to believe all the stories we've been told and our minds compulsively repeat! If you just notice your tendency to rush, and stay committed to slowing down, you will move past this edge quickly. Keep your awareness on your senses. A time may come when you lose track of time and have moments of timeless, direct, and immersive experience. You will know when you are beyond time sickness when the goal you set for time is complete and, instead of wanting to move on to the next thing, you want to linger luxuriantly. Forest bathing is always time well spent.

The Wellspring of Grief

The world is being wounded by humans and our civilizations. As a result we feel deep grief, even if we are usually unaware of it. When we forest bathe, the deep dive into our senses de-anesthetizes us. The emotional impact of grief and trauma we've been suppressing may come to the forefront. These pains are more than personal; they may be the world's pain felt as wounds within our own being. Normally our busy and distracted lives keep us in states of numbness. But when we start connecting deeply with nature in a very personal, intimate way, this grief almost inevitably arises.

Grief is not a disease to be healed, but rather an ally that can guide us in our healing. Support your grief with deep listening. Recognize that your willingness to contact that deep well of sorrow within yourself is a powerful act and it can be a service to others and to the world.

Moments of grieving while forest bathing are usually short-lived, but they are no less profound for their brevity. Be grateful when they appear. Let the forest guide you into a spontaneous grief ceremony, an embodied expression of your sorrow offered as a gift to the world.

Competent As You Are

In forest bathing, there is no rush. No athletic ability is required. I've seen older forest bathers climb carefully into the lower branches of trees and sit there, reconnecting to physical abilities they thought were many years behind them. People who are wheelchair-bound can quietly gaze from a forest sit spot, calling in the medicine that awaits them there. Reconnecting in this way to the eternal inner child, you may have sensory-emotional experiences that are powerfully moving.

Vigilant Awareness

Often people have exaggerated fears of natural hazards. You may be afraid of mountain lions, rattlesnakes, or predatory humans. Some people are afraid to touch plants. It's good to learn what hazards are real and not just imagined and how to be present with them competently without exaggerating or underestimating them. This is one of the ways in which venturing out with a guide is very supportive.

Freedom from the Phone

I hope that you will sometimes leave your cell phone behind when you go forest bathing. The simple act of untethering from our phones can be healing. For many it's definitely a learning edge to leave the phone behind. But because they are profoundly addictive, not having them with us can raise significant anxiety. This is a withdrawal symptom that we can all survive!

But if you do take your cell phone along, here are some suggestions.

Consider putting it on airplane mode, so you can use the camera and perhaps a few other apps without being distracted by communications from the outside world.

Cultivate self-awareness about your motivations for taking photos and how doing so affects your forest experience.

Your phone may have a digital zoom feature that works well as a magnifying glass. Perhaps use this feature one time during your forest bath, then put it away.

Slow-motion video: Of the various videos I've shot on my phone, one of my favorites is a honeybee gathering pollen in slow motion. It looks absolutely drunk in its delight. Time is an elastic concept in the world of nature; a hummingbird's normal speed looks very fast to us! For slow-motion video, choose something that moves quickly.

If your phone has a time-lapse function, mount it on a lightweight portable camera tripod with a phone adapter. Before you cross your Threshold of Connection, find a place off the trail where your camera will be undetected. Point it toward something that will likely move or grow while you are away on your walk. For example, if you are beginning your walk in the morning there may be flowers that closed for the night but will awaken slowly in the first few hours of day. An anthill can be a fascinating subject. Many varieties of mushrooms grow and change rapidly.

After you cross the Threshold of Incorporation, remember to gather your phone. Watch the time-lapse video to see what your phone's camera forest bathing experience was like while you were wandering in liminal space.

7

PRACTICAL MATTERS

Guided or Not Guided?

Forest bathing with a guide is a great way to fully experience this practice and gain an understanding of how to go about it. Guides trained and certified by my colleagues and me have completed a rigorous six-month training course. They intimately know the practice as it is described in this book and much that is not included here. Guides bring considerable skill to offering invitations, facilitating sharing circles, creating thresholds, hosting tea ceremonies, and much more.

It's a bit like yoga. Anyone can stretch, and there are lots of books and videos that explain the asanas (postures) and how to move from each one to the next. But if you really want to be skillful and realize the full benefits of the practice, you will work with a qualified teacher who is credibly certified. The same goes for forest bathing. If at all possible, let a guide introduce you to the practice. Even after you've gained experience, you will benefit from occasionally being guided. As a guide myself, I've found that it is refreshing and essential to sometimes be guided by others.

The perspective of the guide is that the forest is the therapist and the guide's role is to open the doors of the senses. Guides slow you down and help you stay present. They likely have considerable naturalist knowledge, but de-emphasize teaching facts so as to avoid shifting you from your senses back into discursive thought. A trained guide will not try to therapize you. There will be no diagnosis, treatment plan, or therapeutic intervention. They will not impose any spiritual agendas. That will be left for the forest to offer or, more precisely, for you to discover as, tuning in to your senses in new ways, you experience the interface of you and forest.

An excellent resource for finding a guide is the Worldwide Guide Locator Map on the ANFT website at *natureandforesttherapy.earth*. If there are no guides near you, perhaps you will consider becoming one. The website also offers information about guide training and certification programs at the ANFT. You can find out more about the ANFT at the end of this book.

Finding Your Best Places for Forest Bathing

When I travel, I always try to find someplace to forest bathe. I hope you will also. Each forest bathing location and experience illuminates the others. Each forest speaks with its own voice, and together the forests of the world invite us to bathe in their wonderful symphony of sensory and sensual experience.

Suitable places do not always conform to typical ideas of what constitutes a nature trail. I once had a positive "forest bathing" experience in a mall parking lot, where I interacted with a young tree growing in the island between parking areas. Clearly, forests are ideal, but you can make do with what is in your neighborhood. You don't have to be in a forest to do forest bathing.

In the woods, on a path or trail, there are some criteria to consider, and we'll discuss them in the following sections. You may find a wonderful section of trail that meets most of these criteria, while the entire trail does not. If the suitable section is near to a parking area, so much the better. But sometimes you may need to hike for a mile or so to reach your forest bathing site. Or you may have a small garden at home where you can bathe in the company of the plants you love, your cat or dog, and visiting birds. The main rule is to find a place where you can reliably and strongly feel the healing presence of nature.

AN EASE-FULL TRAIL

Ideally, a trail should be close to level. Hills or steep inclines can mean insecure footing, risking injury or physical exertion beyond the capacity of older or physically impaired persons. The trail surface should be reasonably well maintained and free of obstructions that could cause tripping. Of course, if you are forest bathing alone, you can choose trails that match your level of confidence and ability.

SIT SPOTS

There should be pleasant places along the trail to sit and rest with a reasonable degree of solitude. I encourage trail designers to places benches with sit spots in mind. They should be a short distance from the main trail and facing away from it, perhaps partially screened by foliage to give a sense of solitude.

NATIVE PLANTS

In natural settings such as nature preserves or parks, native plants predominate. If you forest bathe in human-built settings, such as botanical gardens, community gardens, and the like, it's nice if at least some native plants are included in the overall mix.

ACCESS TO NATURAL WATERWAYS

Ideally, there is at least one place where people can easily and safely gain access to water and interact with it. A year-round, free-flowing stream with an approachable bank is preferable.

VARIETY OF TERRAIN

There should be a good portion of the trail under forest canopy with a mix of deciduous and evergreen trees and a healthy and diverse understory of species appropriate for the canopy. Having access to a meadow, where the canopy does not interfere with the view of the sky, is also good.

NATURAL SOUNDS

The soundscape is also important, as it comprises a major part of the forest therapy experience. The ideal soundscape consists of entirely natural sounds such as babbling brooks, wind in the trees, birdcalls, and so forth.

BIODIVERSITY

A robust, balanced, and diverse population of birds, mammals, stream inhabitants, and insects lends important qualities to your forest bathing experience. Ideally, herbicides, pesticides, and poisons are absent or only used minimally in the area.

What to Bring

You don't need much gear for forest bathing, and it doesn't have to be expensive outdoor gear, unless the weather calls for it. Do carry a small backpack. Here is a list of things you might want to bring along:

- This book

- Snacks and water or another beverage

- Extra layers, based on expected weather

- If you will be wading in a stream or walking barefoot, flip-flops

- For wading in a stream or slippery conditions, a hiking stick or trekking pole

- For sitting, a small foam pad or a lightweight folding camping stool

- A small first-aid kit for minor injuries

- Sunscreen

- Insect repellent

For your tea ceremony:

- An insulated container for hot water or a backpacking stove to heat water you are carrying

- One cup for each person, plus one for the forest

- A cloth to spread for placing tea cups

- Herbal teas or herbs you have safely gathered along the trail

- Snacks

Depending on how you enjoy using your time, also consider:

- A magnifying glass

- A camera (or a cell phone to use only as a camera)

- Journaling materials

- Materials for making art

- A container for collecting one or two special items found along the way, such as feathers or small stones that appeal to you

- A yoga mat for forest yoga

- Musical instruments

This is not an exhaustive list. Consider what you need, or don't need, for your circumstances and based on your interests.

A Safe Forest Bathing Experience

Fortunately, it is quite rare for someone to be injured during forest bathing walks. Bathers move slowly while paying attention to our environment, and our entire bodies are tuning in to the forest around us. Because of this we are, for example, much more likely to notice when what looks like a stick in the trail is actually a sunbathing rattlesnake. We can then pause and calmly observe and greet it, perhaps offering it a blessing or a song, and then wait for it to move or walk safely around it.

LET SOMEONE KNOW WHERE YOU ARE

Standard outdoor practice is to let someone know where you are going and when you expect to return. Discuss with them what actions to take if you don't return after a specified time.

MAPS AND WHISTLES

If you don't know the area, it's good to have a map. Many parks provide simple trail maps. Your phone likely has a great map function, provided you can get a signal. You can also carry a loud whistle with you; three short blasts on a whistle are a universal distress signal. Repeat every minute or so, while staying in one location so anyone responding can find you quickly.

WEATHER

As all experienced outdoors people know, staying tuned in to weather forecasts is essential. Both heat and cold present their own challenges, as do wet and dry conditions. In high winds I will postpone my forest bath for another day, when the chance of being bonked by a falling limb or tree is not so great. In wet conditions, trails may be more hazardous. That said, some of my favorite walks have been on rainy days. Colors, views, sounds, and smells take on a saturated quality that supports immersive sensory experiences. If you are properly dressed, you can stay warm, mostly dry, and comfortable. In more challenging weather conditions, unless you are very well equipped and experienced, it's probably best to go with a guide. Many forest therapy guides take groups out in snowy conditions with lovely results.

CRITTERS AND PLANTS

Typical hazards encountered along a trail include plants such as poison oak and poison ivy, insects such as wasps who may have nests in the area, venomous snakes, and, of course, mammals feared by many but seen by few, such as mountain lions, wolves, and bears. The list varies depending on your location. Please educate yourself about the potentially harmful plants and animals that live in your neck of the woods.

Where I live on Sonoma Mountain, I sometimes find signs of mountains lions. I wander far afield on this mountain and am usually alone. For a while, I was spooked by the presence of lions, which I never saw but knew were there. One day an experienced tracker asked me, "How many lion attacks have there been around here?" The answer was none. That was a helpful reality check, and I've been much more confident in my wanderings since then.

Tick-borne diseases including Lyme can be a significant hazard. Take ordinary precautions, such as tucking your shirt in and your pants legs into your socks or wearing gaiters. Insect repellents with pyrethrin are said to kill ticks on contact. There are products you can use to impregnate your shoes and pants cuffs with pyrethrin. For sound environmental reasons, many people prefer to not use pyrethrin, choosing alternatives such essential oils.

If you forest bathe in a tick-infested area, make it a routine when you get home to immediately shower and launder the clothes you wore. Then do a tick scan of your hairline along the back of the head, under your arms, and around your groin—favorite spots for the little critters. Learn to recognize ticks, including the tiny nymphs, which may be almost as small as the period at the end of this sentence.

POORLY MAINTAINED TRAILS

Other hazards can result from a combination of inattentiveness while on badly designed or poorly maintained trails. A slope that is a trivial matter in dry conditions can be slippery and hazardous when wet. Look for alternatives; most areas have many trails.

PEOPLE

Unfortunately, another potential hazard is our fellow human beings. It's rare, but sometimes we read about hikers who are victimized by criminals they encounter on a trail or when near a trailhead. We would be naive to think that we are automatically immune from these encounters. There are several commonsense and simple actions we can take to reduce the risks of assault or robbery. If you're concerned about the safety of a particular trail or park, you should consider inviting a friend to come with you or go with a group.

Trust your intuition. If you have a sense of warning or danger, give it your full attention. If you feel a sense of hesitation, hesitate longer, so your awareness has time to process the intuition you are having. In this way, the "knowing" of intuition may transform into conscious understanding. You may remember the odd way that man was standing near the map at the trailhead, the beat-up car you noticed at the far end of the lot, or the broken beer bottle you saw without noticing as you drove up the road—all caught in the net of your subconscious awareness. Intuitively you recognize a pattern that is important. The inner voice of intuition always speaks for your best interests. Give it heed.

8

FOREST BATHING IN JAPAN

Forest bathing in Japan is remarkably like the form I've described in this book. There are also some differences. I'm sure this would be true in any other country where forest bathing has been developed by local enthusiasts. I'll describe here a few features of forest bathing in Japan I find most intriguing.

Guides

The guides I've met in Japan are all highly trained professionals. Typical guide-training courses are about a year in duration. The design of the Japanese training program is like that of the ANFT, combining intensive field-based training periods with a practicum that includes a supervised curriculum to deepen guide trainees' skills and knowledge. All guides are required to have first-aid certification at a level like that required of ANFT-certified guides, who must keep current certification in Wilderness First Aid.

Weekend Getaways

The Japanese have developed a series of designated forest bathing trails and forest healing centers. These are located in rural areas, near towns where there are hotels and other amenities. The towns are all accessible by train or bus. Many Japanese make forest bathing a part of weekend getaways. They leave the cities and come to the mountains for relaxation and to restore their energy and focus. Some corporations in Japan subsidize these weekend getaways as part of their employee wellness strategies. Overwork and stress-induced illness are well-recognized phenomena in Japan. The Japanese word *karoshi* refers to death by overwork. The practice of shinrin-yoku is woven into a nationwide response to this concern. Many of the more than 140,000 annual visitors to the Akazawa Healing Forest travel there for the purpose of shinrin-yoku.

Infrastructure

The trails I visited in Japan were extremely well designed and maintained. Many were specifically built for forest bathing. For example, one of the trails at Okutama begins with a gentle series of switchbacks that climb a short distance. At the top there are benches built at an angle for nighttime stargazing. For those who are wheelchair-bound or who need extra assistance, a lift carries them up a rail system to the top of the grade, where the trail levels out. A series of decks have been constructed along the hillside trail here, where forest bathers can sit and gaze into the forest from about the mid-height of the trees.

On this trail, you make a one-way journey and are met by a shuttle at the end. The trail begins at a beautiful small office building where your guides greet you and assist you with measuring your blood pressure and salivary amylase. You make notes of the results and carry them with you to compare to readings at the end. About a kilometer up the trail, you come to a lovely small building with an indoor amphitheater-style room where you can sit and gaze through large windows. This building has a wood-burning stove, a small kitchen, and restrooms—a very inviting space.

Continuing along the trail, you pass many benches and eventually come to a series of large wooden platforms. A yoga instructor meets you and guides you through a gentle series of poses. A bit farther along, you come to another cabin. Here you take your blood pressure and measure salivary amylase again and compare the results with the first set of measurements.

Health Care

Forest therapy guides in Japan are working to integrate the practice with medical systems, but have not yet succeeded. However, shinrin-yoku can accurately be described as part of the health care system. It flourishes in the domain of personal health and wellness choices, where along with exercise, good nutrition, supportive social networks, and the like, it is taking root for many Japanese as part of a healthy lifestyle. Forest bathing is widely recognized as an effective disease prevention strategy.

CONCLUSION:
AWAKENING THE WILD

So, what should we make of forest bathing? Specifically, what is the reason for its emergence in these times? We see it developing in many countries, in many forms. This is a sign of what I call an "earth dreaming." Somehow, the earth is dreaming this work into being, spreading it like the seeds of a dandelion. Many of these seeds are taking root. What is its purpose in calling us back into the forests?

Some theological writings refer to the phrase *crown of creation*, which relates to the idea that humans are made in the image of God and we alone of all creation share certain characteristics with God. Sentience is one of these. In this view no other aspect of creation has the ability to feel, perceive, or experience subjectively—to have sentience. Thus, we are given dominion over the earth and all creation. The essence of this dominion is a duty to subdue and bring the whole of the more-than-human world into an order that reflects God's glory and will.

That plan isn't working out so well. Dominion becomes *domination*, a trait of the wounded masculine. This is antithetical to the *partnership* trait of the healing feminine. Domination is a recipe for broken relationship and perpetual cycles of trauma. The time has come to abandon our dominator orientation to subjugation and exploitation of each other and the land. We must learn to be dancers, not dominators, or we will surely come to know what it is to perish. The forests offer us their support for this necessary learning journey.

What if our special role as humans is dominion in a different sense: that of understanding the scope or domain of our species' role in the great family of beings? The trees have been planting within me this question: what if being in the "image of God" means that we have the ability—and responsibility—to nurture the sentience of other beings, to help wake them up? Perhaps the earth is asking us to be bringers of reveille, agents of awakening, calling forth the full conscious potential of creation, so it too can do its work. As in the fairy tale of sleeping beauty, there is a kiss that awakens the sleeper. Forest bathers bestow this awakening kiss when we cultivate softhearted, sensual, connective, and communicative relationships with the trees and streams, the stones and sky, and all the many beings.

But even this idea falls short. For ultimately, we are not the ones who call the trees to awakening. We are calling to awaken each other. It not just the sleeping beauty who is awakened at the moment of the kiss; the one who kisses also comes into a greater fullness of life. It is a deep kiss, a meeting beyond reciprocity. More than an exchange between two separate beings: it is a remembering of our oneness. Our partnership with forest and the whole of the more-than-human world is a necessary thread on the loom of the evolution of the world. We have a place we are called to inhabit in the family of things. It is my prayer that we can do so well, with the grace and beauty and power we have been given. If our species fails, if we fall into extinction, the forests will grieve but they will continue, and over the vast spans of time another species will be called forth to take our place.

May we overcome our cleverness and find our wisdom. The trees offer us a bridge to our own wisdom; their listening does not call forth ideas of greed and exploitation, but of beauty and familial membership. For me, forest bathing leads ever deeper toward embodied knowing, beyond doubt, of my interbeing with the forest, with all beings, and with the family of all the inhabitants of the more-than-human world. May it be so for you as well.

SONOMA MOUNTAIN
DECEMBER 2017

PRACTICES AND REFLECTIONS

These invitations are designed to be practiced in any outdoor setting—whether it be a forest, a patch of woods in your neighborhood, or even your backyard. With each invitation, space is included for taking notes of your experiences. Or better yet, use a notebook as your forest bathing journal. These invitations can be downloaded here *http://bit.ly/Invitations_to_Forest_Bathing* and printed to pack in your bag and take with you.

Sit Spot

Sit spot is a very simple yet powerful practice. It can be practiced in any natural setting and even on your front porch or a park bench. The emphasis should be on ease and practicality. Aim to visit this spot frequently, daily, if possible. When you sit quietly for half an hour, some kind of story will usually unfold: a bird swoops down and lands nearby, squirrels chase each other up a tree, the wind stirs the leaves . . . .

- *Choose a place you can visit frequently and without too much effort.*
- *Sit quietly for thirty minutes.*
- *What story is unfolding?*
- *How is this spot different from the last time you visited it?*

_____

_____

_____

_____

_____

_____

_____

_____

Wander

This simple invitation can be done in any natural area or even in a park—any place that has trails or paths you can easily follow and just wander.

- *Be relaxed and move slowly.*
- *Remember that this is an invitation, not an assignment or exercise.*
- *Allow yourself to be carried away from time to time by scents and sounds or desires to touch or smell things you may pass.*
- *What are you noticing?*

_____

_____

_____

_____

_____

_____

_____

_____

_____

_____

_____

_____

_____

_____

_____

_____

_____

_____

_____

_____

_____

_____

_____

_____

_____

_____

_____

_____

_____

_____

_____

_____

_____

_____

_____

_____

_____

Gesture

The natural world communicates with you through sensory experience. This practice provides a way to communicate back.

- *Close your eyes and slowly turn in a circle, noticing which direction you feel drawn to.*
- *When you have decided, open your eyes and simply gaze in that direction. Gaze with your whole being . . . your eyes, your heart, your body.*
- *Notice any feelings that arise—of wonder, gratitude, joy, or, from other directions, tension or anxiety.*
- *Make a gesture to express what you are feeling. You might bow, raise your hands, or even dance or sing.*
- *Listen quietly for a response. What do you hear?*
- *What feelings arise?*

_____

_____

_____

_____

_____

_____

_____

Your Guide to Forest Bathing

_____

_____

_____

_____

_____

_____

_____

_____

_____

_____

_____

_____

_____

_____

_____

_____

_____

_____

_____

_____

_____

_____

_____

Place Tending

I have been tending a small redwood grove near my house for several years. I pick up trash, keep track of which birds are nesting where, and talk to visitors when I encounter them. But I also simply spend time in the grove and give this place the gift of loving human company.

- *Choose a place near your home that needs tending and visit it frequently. It can be a small corner of your yard, or even a planter on your apartment's balcony.*
- *Touch the trees or plants.*
- *Notice how the weather and the seasons change this place over time.*
- *How is this place different from the last time you visited?*

_____

_____

_____

_____

_____

_____

_____

_____

_____

_____

_____

_____

_____

_____

_____

_____

_____

_____

_____

_____

_____

_____

_____

_____

_____

_____

_____

_____

_____

_____

_____

Practices and Reflections

Gratitude Altar

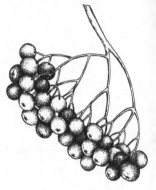

At the place you tend or in a special place you discover while wandering, build a small altar to express your gratitude.

- *Collect some natural items such as sticks, stones, feathers, flowers, ferns, and any other beautiful but impermanent things you find. Arrange these items creatively.*

- *Make it a practice to maintain your altar by rebuilding and reshaping it each time you visit.*

- *What are you grateful for in this moment? Think of something that is immediate and tangibly present, such as the sound of the birds or the scent on the breeze.*

_____

_____

_____

_____

_____

_____

_____

_____

_____

_____

_____

_____

_____

_____

_____

_____

_____

_____

_____

_____

_____

_____

_____

_____

_____

_____

_____

_____

_____

_____

_____

Self-Portrait

Having a hard time leaving your phone behind when you go on a forest bathing walk? Here's a way to put it to good use. This practice can help bring something into focus that you might not have been able to see on your own. Just be sure to silence your calls and notifications!

- *Wander in a wooded or natural area for about fifteen minutes. Look for natural things that remind you of some aspect of yourself or your life as it is now.*

- *Photograph a few of these examples.*

- *Pick the photo that best represents an aspect of yourself or your life in this moment and write about it. Describe it in detail. What is it about the elements or their composition that drew you to them?*

- *After you're finished writing, put your phone away and continue with your walk.*

_____

_____

_____

_____

_____

_____

_____

_____

_____

_____

_____

_____

_____

_____

_____

_____

_____

_____

_____

_____

_____

_____

_____

_____

_____

_____

_____

_____

_____

_____

Stethostones

Stones can be used much like stethoscopes to hear what is going in inside trees and even in the earth below us. Not all stones work effectively. So, part of this invitation is to experiment by trying a few different stones until you find one that works for you.

- *Find a stone that fits comfortably in the palm of your hand and is smooth on both sides. River stones are good candidates.*

- *Place the stone at the height of your ear against the trunk of a young tree, no more than six inches in diameter. Lean your ear into the stone. Allow your breathing and your mind to become quiet; this may take a minute or two.*

- *As you become quiet inside, what sounds do you notice coming through your "stethoscope"? Describe them. What do the sounds remind you of?*

_____

_____

_____

_____

_____

_____

_____

_____

_____

_____

_____

_____

_____

_____

_____

_____

_____

_____

_____

_____

_____

_____

_____

_____

_____

_____

_____

_____

_____

_____

_____

Try this . . .

Sometimes an invitation will appear on its own.
It's as if the land itself is whispering, "Try this . . ."
Listen carefully for these whispers; they are the
voice of your sense of knowing. Often they appear
as questions like, "Wouldn't it be fun to try . . .", or,
"I wonder what happens if. . . ." If one of these questions arises, let go of
what you might have planned and follow your curiosity.

- *Where or what are you called to?*

- *Which of your senses is leading you?*

- *How are your senses helping to connect you with the place where you are?*

_____

_____

_____

_____

_____

_____

_____

_____

_____

NOTES

1. Henry David Thoreau, "Walking," *Atlantic Magazine* (June 1862): *https://www.theatlantic.com/magazine/archive/1862/06/walking/304674/*.

2. Ming Kuo, "How Might Contact with Nature Promote Human Health? Promising Mechanisms and a Possible Central Pathway." *Frontiers in Psychology* 6 (August 2015).

3. Margaret M. Hanson, Reo Jones, and Kirsten Tocchini. "Shinrin-Yoku (Forest Bathing) and Nature Therapy: A State-of-the-Art Review." *International Journal of Environmental Research and Public Health*, 14, 851 (2017).

4. M. Kat Anderson, *Tending the Wild: Native American Knowledge and the Management of California's Natural Resources* (Berkeley: University of California Press, 2005).

5. Shunryu Suzuki, *Zen Mind, Beginner's Mind* (Boston: Shambhala Publications, 2006).

6. Larry Dossey, MD, *Space, Time and Medicine* (Boston: Shambhala Publications, 1982).

RESOURCES

Recommended Reading

Ackerman, Diane. *A Natural History of the Senses*. New York: Random House, 1990.

A celebration of the senses.

Beresford-Kroeger, Diana. *The Global Forest*. New York: Viking, 2010.

A love song to forests.

Berry, Thomas. *The Great Work: Our Way into the Future*. New York: Bell Tower, 1999.

This is why we do this work.

Buhner, Stephen Harrod. *Plant Intelligence and the Imaginal Realm: Beyond the Doors of Perception into the Dreaming Earth*. Rochester, Vt.: Bear and Company, 2014.

One of the foremost practitioners and philosophers of herbal medicine shares his experience and insights on communicating with plants.

Hackenmiller, Suzanne Bartlett, MD. *The Outdoor Adventurer's Guide to Forest Bathing*. Guilford, CT: Falcon Guides, 2019.

Forest bathing practices tailored to your favorite activities.

Hall, Matthew. *Plants as Persons: A Philosophical Botany*. Albany, N.Y.: SUNY Press, 2011.

An exploration of how, why, and when humanity lost sight of the sentience of trees and other plants.

Louv, Richard. *The Nature Principle: Human Restoration and the End of Nature-Deficit Disorder*. Chapel Hill, N.C.: Algonquin Books of Chapel Hill, 2011.

A comprehensive recounting of the ways in which practitioners of nature connection are being guided by science to help us take back from industrial medicine our own paths to well-being.

Trotta, R. Michael. *Sit Spot and the Art of Inner Tracking: A 30-Day Challenge to Develop Your Relationship to Self, Others, Earth, and the Wisdom of the Ancients*. n.p.: CreateSpace Independent Publishing Platform, 2014.

For those who want to cultivate sit spots, this book has a thirty-day program to build skills and sharpen the ability to connect deeply with nature.

Williams, Florence. *The Nature Fix: Why Nature Makes Us Happier, Healthier, and More Creative*. New York: W. W. Norton and Company, 2017.

Florence Williams announced shinrin-yoku to the Western world in a 2012 article in *Outside Magazine*. Now she has given us a beautiful collection of the science and research at the forefront of helping us understand the imperative to include nature in how we live.

Wohllenben, Peter. *The Hidden Life of Trees: What They Feel, How They Communicate: Discoveries from a Secret World*. Vancouver, B.C., and Berkeley, Calif.: Greystone Books, 2016.

This book reviews the science that is revealing the sensory complexity and sentience of trees and the importance of intact forest ecosystems.

Young, Jon. *What the Robin Knows: How Birds Reveal the Secrets of the Natural World*. Boston: Houghton Mifflin Harcourt, 2013.

Recommended Films

Miyazaki, Hayao. *My Neighbor Totoro*. Tokyo: Studio Ghibli, 1988.

———. *Princess Mononoke*. Tokyo: Studio Ghibli, 1997.

———. *Spirited Away*. Tokyo: Studio Ghibli, 2001.

These films share stories for the inner child in each of us, exploring the secret spirit ecologies of forests and their connection with humans.

An Online Resource for Forest Bathers

Natureandforesttherapy.earth provides up-to-date information on developments related to forest bathing. Here you can find:

- Training opportunities to become a guide
- A map to help you find qualified guides and forest bathing instructors near you
- A schedule of the author's training and lecture appearances
- An invitation to join the email list for occasional updates and to stay notified of forest bathing opportunities
- Links to many online resources

I hope forest bathing will become a familiar part of your wellness promotion and disease prevention strategies. To this end, my colleagues and I continue our work to build a global network of trained forest bathing and forest therapy guides and teachers.

ABOUT THE AUTHOR

M. Amos Clifford is a leading voice for Shinrin-Yoku inspired Forest Therapy in the United States. He is the founder of the Association of Nature and Forest Therapy Guides and Programs, an organization leading the movement to integrate nature and forest therapies into health care, education, and land management systems. He has been a student of Buddhist philosophy for over twenty years and is the founder of Sky Creek Dharma Center in Chico, CA. Visit Amos at *natureandforesttherapy.earth*.